ADVANCE PRAISE FOR **HR ON PURPOSE**

"Steve does a masterful job of not only helping us all understand what capabilities are needed to be successful into the future in our profession, but does so in a manner that leaves us excited, inspired, and ready to take action. *HR on Purpose* is a must-read for anyone at any point in their career in the ever-changing HR field."

!! Jason Averbook, *Co-founder of Infusion and former CEO, The Marcus Buckingham Company*

"Steve Browne has a passage in this book that says: 'When you go into a grocery store, you are drawn to the things that are placed to catch your eye. Companies intentionally pay for better shelf space so that you will look at their brands in the hope that you're more likely to buy their goods. We have to do this in HR. We have to get in the line of sight of our employees and make our goods attractive and accessible.' I urge you to put this book at eye level in wherever you work and make sure you see this book every day. Each day, open it like an HR daily devotional and read for five minutes. It doesn't really matter where you open the book. Just randomly open it and read. You will be a better HR professional and a better person for doing it."

!! Paul Hebert, *Senior Director, Solutions Architecture, Creative Group*

"As someone who has known Steve Browne for many years and considers him a friend and mentor, I've been suggesting for years that he write a book to share his wealth of wisdom and experiences with HR and business leaders. I'm so excited that it's finally here! This book is a great collection of personal stories and observations, as well as great tips and advice for human resources professionals. Steve's encouragement to engage with people, get to know them, and make HR relevant in the workplace is much needed, and his guidance and strategies come both from years of experience as a successful HR/business/community leader and from the heart. He truly cares about the future of HR and HR professionals. I strongly suggest that you read this book and highlight relevant passages so you can refer and continually challenge yourself to implement the suggestions that are offered. If you want to be encouraged, inspired, and given a road map for success as an HR professional, this book is a must-read!"

!! Jennifer McClure, *President, Unbridled Talent LLC, and CEO, DisruptHR LLC*

"Steve Browne reminds us of the rewards of a career in human resources. He shares his wisdom and experiences, and underscores the importance of focusing on others first and always. Not just because it's a feel-good idea, but because it's an effective way to influence business and affect the bottom line."

!! Susan Meisinger, *SHRM-SCP, SPHR, J.D., former CEO of SHRM and renowned columnist on HR leadership*

"If you're looking for an HR leadership role model, look no further than Steve Browne. *HR on Purpose* is your opportunity to be mentored by one of the best in the profession. No matter where you are in your career, this book offers a fresh perspective and a challenge to collectively improve our craft. This book is a potent mentoring tool and a constant reminder of the importance of HR in organizations."
!! Sharlyn Lauby, *SHRM-SCP, President at ITM Group Inc. and author of the HR Bartender blog*

"In *HR on Purpose*, Steve Browne confidently illustrates the importance of practicing HR intentionally. Brimming with humor, Browne provides vivid anecdotes that highlight and underlie the practical points he is making. It is not the HR book we deserve, but the HR book we need."
!! Matthew Stollak, *SHRM-SCP, SPHR, Associate Professor of Business Administration, St. Norbert College*

"This is an exceptional, easy read with practical and actionable advice. I found myself laughing, nodding in agreement and wanting to immediately share this with my students and my professional network. Steve's examples and writing are magnificent. If you're new to the profession or an accomplished pro, you will be 'geeked' about HR after reading Steve's book!"
!! John P. Nykolaiszyn, *SHRM-SCP, Director, Career Management Services, College of Business, Florida International University*

"Steve is one of the bright lights in our profession and professional organization. His insights into our profession are spot-on, and his enthusiasm for it is unsurpassed. *HR on Purpose* will inspire many HR professionals both in the field and working with SHRM."
!! John K. Jorgensen, *SHRM-SCP, SPHR, Principal, JKJ HR*

"Steve reminds me of my dear mom in that he teaches through storytelling. And, just like my mom, he turns the lesson into a joyful experience. Each one of his chapters has a funny yet poignant story that, if we're paying attention and drawing our inferences, inspires us to become better, more valuable HR professionals and leaders."
!! Heather Kinzie, *SHRM-SCP, SPHR, GPHR, Partner, The Strive Group*

"Steve Browne is the most positive and dynamic force in real-life HR leadership. *HR on Purpose* will entertain and inform any HR professional or line manager. Buy this book if you want to get a glimpse of the bright future of HR leadership or if you want to share his wise human resource management counsel with your company managers."
!! Franny Oxford, *SHRM-SCP, SPHR, MA, Vice President of HR, Five Star Management*

HR ON PURPOSE

PURPOSE

DEVELOPING DELIBERATE PEOPLE PASSION

STEVE BROWNE

HR ON PURPOSE

DEVELOPING DELIBERATE PEOPLE PASSION

STEVE BROWNE

Society for Human Resource Management
Alexandria, Virginia
www.shrm.org

Strategic Human Resource Management India
Mumbai, India
www.shrmindia.org

Society for Human Resource Management
Haidian District Beijing, China
www.shrm.org/cn

Society for Human Resource Management, Middle East and Africa Online
Dubai, UAE
www.shrm.org/pages/mena.aspx

SOCIETY FOR HUMAN
RESOURCE MANAGEMENT

This publication is designed to provide accurate and authoritative information regarding the subject matter covered. It is sold with the understanding that neither the publisher nor the author is engaged in rendering legal or other professional service. If legal advice or other expert assistance is required, the services of a competent, licensed professional should be sought. The federal and state laws discussed in this book are subject to frequent revision and interpretation by amendments or judicial revisions that may significantly affect employer or employee rights and obligations. Readers are encouraged to seek legal counsel regarding specific policies and practices in their organizations.

This book is published by the Society for Human Resource Management (SHRM). The interpretations, conclusions, and recommendations in this book are those of the author and do not necessarily represent those of the publisher.

SHRM books and products are available on most online bookstores and through the SHRMStore at www.shrmstore.org.

The Society for Human Resource Management is the world's largest HR professional society, representing 290,000 members in more than 165 countries. For nearly seven decades, the Society has been the leading provider of resources serving the needs of HR professionals and advancing the practice of human resource management. SHRM has more than 575 affiliated chapter within the United States and subsidiary offices in China, India, and United Arab Emirates. Please visit us at www.shrm.org.

Interior & Cover Design	Katerina B. Cochran
Manager, Creative Services	James McGinnis
Manager, Book Publishing	Matthew Davis
Vice President, Editorial	Tony Lee

Library of Congress Cataloging-in-Publication Data has been applied for and is on file with the Library of Congress.

ISBN (pbk): 978-1-586-44425-9; ISBN (ePDF): 978-1-586-44426-6; ISBN (ePUB): 978-1-586-44427-3; ISBN (eMobi): 978-1-586-44428-0

Printed in the United States of America
FIRST EDITION

PB Publishing   10 9 8 7 6

17-0053 | 61.15018

DEDICATION

I'd like to dedicate this book to my amazing wife, Debbie, and my incredible kids, Melanie and Josh. You have always been supportive of my quirky habits, love of music, lava lamps, and tie-dye. I wouldn't have had the career in HR that I've had without you in my life. I'm very thankful for you and love you to the ends of the world!!

CONTENTS

ACKNOWLEDGEMENTS

No one ever accomplishes anything in their career without some amazing people along the way. First of all, thanks to my Mom and Dad who have always expected the best from me and everyone they've encountered throughout life. You set an incredible example of great humans who happen to also be my parents. I would be remiss if I didn't thank the professors at Ohio University who helped shape and mold my view of people in a holistic way. OU will always be my home away from home.

As for my career, thanks to Richard Morris who took a kid who left a *Fortune* 100 company and gave me a chance to be his HR generalist. You taught me the intrinsic value that resided in ALL employees. I am forever grateful for the chance you took on me and for this priceless advice. Thanks to Becky Eisenmann and Kathy Coleman who showed me leadership through grace. You both have been essential in showing me how to live, thrive and succeed in a workplace. Thanks to Kevin Burrill, Michael LaRosa, and Mark LaRosa who took another chance and allowed me to become the HR professional I've always wanted to become. I don't take one thing for granted with these people and the countless employees I've worked with and for so far throughout my career.

Finally, thanks to the HR community of Cincinnati, Ohio, and the Greater Cincinnati HR Association. You have been a significant factor in molding me and allowing me to grow professionally within human resources as an industry. After becoming a chapter member and being fortunate enough to be the chapter president, countless doors have opened so that I could be a volunteer leader locally as well as for the entire state of Ohio and then for the entire country through SHRM. I am grateful that I am a part of your fabric. Please know that you will always be a part of mine.

FOREWORD

Dear Reader,

Chances are you have chosen to read this book because you are an HR professional, want to be in human resources, you know the author, have read his work online, or you want to be inspired in your work.

Regardless of the path that led you to crack open the cover, it is my hope that you laugh out loud as you experience the personal anecdotes sprinkled across the pages, that you make time to ponder how to approach the work you do and why you do it, and that you share this book with a colleague.

Between the familiar scenarios and the funny situations, you will be presented with questions. These are purposefully geared toward you as a means to help you with your own personal development and career. I challenge you to make time to reflect and answer honestly—you will be happy you did!

It is my opinion that human resources is the heartbeat of any organization. It is not just a department made up of many functions within it, but it truly is the **HUMANS** working for your company. While it is vital for us as HR practitioners to be connected to business operations and understand how our organizations make money, it is equally important that we be an advocate for the people for whom we work. That is why it is critical that we do this work with passion and purpose.

Enjoy these words of wisdom from one of the kindest humans, and brightest lights, on the face of the earth!!

Tiffany Kuehl, SHRM-CP

P.S. Llamas

INTRODUCTION

MOST PEOPLE DON'T THINK ABOUT their work as a career or even a choice. I would venture to say that most see work as tedious or as a necessary means to be able to provide for themselves and others. I don't hear many people talk about their work with joy and passion. Why is that? If we spend the majority of our time here on this planet in some vocation, why would approaching it with dread and frustration be a good thing?

What if people looked at their work as a choice that they made intentionally? That's not easy, and some may feel it's impossible. It usually isn't a choice that comes easy. There is a path people travel, and they run into some obstacles, and even failures, before they land in the field that fits them.

I grew up in the small village, yes "village," of Ada, Ohio. The best way to describe my hometown is that it was very much like the town of Mayberry from "The Andy Griffith Show." Everyone knows everyone in Ada. It was a great environment to be in. I loved school and was fortunate to graduate as co-valedictorian in a booming class of 73 students.

Being the valedictorian meant that people, including me, assumed that I would pursue a career in an academically challenging field like engineering. So I trekked to Ohio University (OU) to become a chemical engineer. It made sense to me because I could apply my love of math and science as a job.

That lasted one quarter. I was not wired to be an engineer.

I didn't want to disappoint people back home, so I switched my major to chemistry. As I continued in my classes, my grades kept plummeting. I was miserable.

The tipping point came one day during a chem lab when my lab partner and I were conducting an experiment. He was sick and shouldn't have come to class. We were working with benzene, which is a potential carcinogen. I looked across the lab desk, and my friend was clammy and dripping with sweat. The last thing he needed to be around was benzene!!

I begged the professor to let my lab partner go home to take care of himself, and I even offered to come in over the weekend to redo the experiment with him. On a side note—my lab partner was an honors tutorial student in chemistry with a 4.0 GPA in every class. Missing one lab experiment wasn't going to hurt him. The professor told me to "mind my own business and do my work." I told the professor he was wrong and I was taking my friend back to his dorm. The professor was furious that I was being defiant. I didn't care. He told me that if we left, we'd fail the lab. I didn't care. We left.

One other thing to know about me—I'm not very good with authority or conformity, but I'll cover this later.

My lab partner made up the lab and got another A, and the professor followed through and gave me an F as he promised. I asked him why he was inconsistent, and he threatened to kick me out of his class. That quarter I stopped being a chemistry major. I was also put on academic probation and was on the verge of flunking out of college altogether.

I went back to Ada over the break crushed. I had never struggled or failed in anything—especially academically. I was lost and not sure what to do. One night my mom (who is amazing by the way!!) encouraged me to get out the OU catalog and review the majors the university had to offer. I was reluctant and ashamed. My mom wasn't fazed and sat down with me.

Without missing a beat she asked, "Steve, do you know that you're **ALWAYS** surrounded by people?" I didn't know what she meant.

She continued, "You don't see it do you? Ever since you've been young, you're in the midst of people. In your activities at school, at church, in the community—you're never alone. Why don't you look for something as a career where you can be with people all the time? Find something where you can be who you really are."

What she said made sense, and I felt so much better. At OU I worked as a resident assistant, participated on several intramural teams, was active at church, and was immersed in the Athens, Ohio, community. I thumbed through the catalog (pre-Internet days) and came across a major called "interpersonal communication." I made the switch and threw myself into classes that dealt with all facets of people and how they interact.

One class I ended up taking was Interviewing, and the final project was for everyone to interview classmates and to be interviewed personally. The students had to vote for which person was the best interviewer and which person was the best interviewee. They voted that I should interview myself!! It was the sign I was hoping for.

College wrapped up, and I graduated with a Bachelor's degree in interpersonal communications and a minor in chemistry, and I added another minor in history because history is just cool. I also worked hard enough to graduate with honors. The next step was the career choice and I chose … human resources.

This was a new term when I entered the field. It had been "personnel" for decades. The great thing about this career choice that "fit" is that I've been in HR on purpose ever since.

It's the only field I've experienced and the only one I will ever be in. Why? Because I get to be with people—on purpose—every day. I have to have that. It energizes me in ways that are visible, tangible, and relevant.

In this book, I will show you how you can be in HR on purpose!! It's a way to show you that being in human resources has value both personally and professionally. It's an industry in which you can touch people's lives in meaningful ways as well as drive entire organizations forward.

As you go through the book, I want you to experience what I did when I had to change and make a decision with my major. I hope you find value, clarity, and excitement so that you enjoy who you are and what you do as an HR professional.

Now, you'll see some unconventional approaches here and there, and you may see words like "geeked" and a lot of double exclamation points!! This isn't for show or to motivate you in some shallow way. It's how I see HR, and I won't apologize for it being a bit irreverent and against the rules and norms of how people are supposed to write.

So, if you're willing, I want you to drop the filters and preconceptions of what HR *should* be and take a look instead into what HR *could* be!! Ready?? I am ... and I'm **GEEKED!!**

CHAPTER 1

ALL APOLOGIES

BEFORE WE PROCEED any further, I have to come clean about something. I am a music freak!! I have music playing in every environment I can and for as much of the day as I can. During the 1990s MTV aired an incredible series called "MTV Unplugged." This series featured acts that were a mix of classic rock legends and artists who were popular at the time. One of my favorite episodes featured Nirvana. The band was at the height of its popularity and hearing its usually raucous and loud music stripped down made me fall for the band even more. One song the group performed was "All Apologies," and it was haunting.

Hearing Kurt Cobain sing with such pain and angst just drew me into the song. I felt the deep emotions he was trying to communicate, and it made me think of ... HR!!

If people outside of human resources described our field, they would say that we were magnificent apologists. We apologize for who we are and what we do way too often. It sounds a lot like this conversation overheard at a networking event:

"Hi, how are you?"

"Fine and you?"

"I'm good. I'm Steve and you are?"

"Melanie."

"Nice to meet you, Melanie. Where do you work, and what do you do?"

"I work for a local manufacturer, and I'm one of their salespeople. And you?"

"I work in the restaurant industry, and I'm in human resources."

"Oh, sorry."

"It's okay. I like being in HR."

"Really? Most HR people I know don't say that."

Encouraging, isn't it? You're out trying to establish professional connections, and others view your profession as something that needs an apology. When did we allow this to happen? Which HR professionals thought that taking this approach would make their position strong either personally or professionally? I don't know if there's a "person zero" responsible for this apology movement, but more HR people have adopted this stance than have tried to dispel it.

HR is tough. There is no denying it. When you look at the breadth of the field of human resources, it's daunting. When a person is tasked with being knowledgeable in employee relations, recruiting, compensation, benefits, employment law, federal and state regulations, training, organizational development, etc., all at the same time, one can see how the job could be overwhelming. I know these tasks describe HR practitioners who are generalists, but even specialists have very broad roles that touch these same areas in some aspect on a regular basis. Where we have lost perspective is that ALL fields in business are tough.

If you asked someone in marketing to break down his or her field, you'd see that it's also filled with diversity, complexity, and depth. The difference in other fields and ours is that we have taken the stance of being a martyr who experiences untold levels of suffering to meet the common good of the people. There is one differentiator in human resources that not all other business roles have, and that is the direct interaction with people. The odd thing about this differentiator is that the people who are most often vocal and frustrated with employees in organizations work in HR!!

If this describes you, then please take this advice. If employees are a pain point or source of frustration for you professionally, then get out of human resources. It isn't the career for you.

Quit trying to tough it out because you are this administrative superstar who can make systems hum. Administration is an important facet of HR, but it is not the reason we exist. Without people we are nothing. Please note that this isn't the call for you to put the "H" back into HR. That is a popular sentiment that you'll hear speakers share during presentations or as the theme of an HR blog. It's become a catch phrase without context and a shallow self-help statement to make us feel better. Whenever I hear someone throw this out, my quick retort is "The 'H' in HR? You mean 'Hell'??"

It throws people, and I don't mean it, just as they don't actually mean what they say either. Working with people has to be more than a feel-good catch phrase. The reality that we are intimately intertwined with people is exciting, not frustrating.

It's time for you to own who you are as an HR professional. There is value in what you do for your organization and for the people who work there. Human resources brings life to a company. With that being the case, why would you ever apologize for being a part of this field?

Much of what we do hinges on two things—our perspective and our approach. So, before we move forward and dive deep into how HR can really exist for you in a fresh, vibrant, and relevant way, you need to stop being an apologist. Step back, look at what you do, and **OWN it!!** HR rocks on so many levels, and it needs to be expressed through you and not in spite of you.

CHAPTER 2

30 DAYS ... OR ELSE

MY HR CAREER started like most in recruiting. It's a great place to get your feet wet because you're learning the front end of the employee cycle. It's also a bit daunting because you're in the middle of making sure that the hiring managers get their positions filled on a timely basis and that the candidates have a good experience as they're being considered. I worked for a large *Fortune* 100 company that was extremely traditional and conservative in all of its business practices. This ran so deep that there was even an internal dictionary of acronyms to be used in all interoffice communication that was an inch thick!!

Given that it was my first HR role, I did whatever was asked of me, and I took on each opportunity with fervor. It was a bit uncomfortable for me to be in a highly specialized role because I was more comfortable having a broader scope. I was learning what it was like to work and also exploring what mattered to me personally within a human resource job. I didn't know what it meant to be an HR generalist or that this type of position even existed. I was ignorant of the power of culture in an organization because companies weren't talking about, or concerned with, culture The focus of organizations was that work was to get done, and that was it. I wasn't aware of the broader HR community or that other people around the world practiced HR.

You shouldn't be surprised by this. My first HR role was before the Internet was around, and I joined the workforce when the main measurements of your performance were that you showed up to work, didn't rock the boat, and did what you were told. Unfortunately, when I look over the work landscape currently, many of these measurements still are the drivers in many organizations.

I enjoyed my time in my first role for a while. Over time it became more and more evident that I didn't fit the corporate world. Keep in mind that this company was, and still is, incredibly successful. The reality that I didn't fit it didn't matter much to its ongoing success. I chose to leave and venture into something that I hoped would fit better. Never one to follow the easiest path, my next role was for an entrepreneurial startup.

Culture shock occurred literally the first day I started with this new organization. After I completed the obligatory new-hire paperwork, I had a face-to-face meeting with the company's founder and CEO. He welcomed me, and then he threw down the gauntlet.

"Steve, do you know why we hired you?"

"You hired me to take care of human resources for the company."

"No, not really."

I admit that I was confused by this. I was very excited to have an opportunity to become the HR focus for this startup. I wasn't quite sure what he expected of me, and then he hit me with a monumental challenge.

"I have an assignment for you to get you started here. You have 30 days to complete this. I want you to learn all employees in the company by name, where they work, and what they do. On the 30th day, you and I will meet here again and I'll quiz you. If you get one person wrong, you'll be fired. Do you understand the assignment?"

I gulped and said, "Yes sir," and that was the end of our meeting on my first day. I sat at the conference room table for some time trying to gauge whether this conversation really happened. He was serious. This was not some ploy or truth-or-dare scenario. He gave me an assignment, and I had a 30-day deadline. At the time of this challenge, we had a corporate office and three manufacturing locations that ran two shifts (two in Ohio and one in South Carolina) with a total of 225 employees. On top of this, I didn't have a computer at my desk, and a laptop was some mythical invention that was just starting to be a part of the business world!!

To get started, I went old school and started reading every personnel folder in the office. It took me several days just to get through this mountain of information. Then, I did something completely radical (even though I didn't know it at the time) and went to our plants to meet the employees. I met with every single person on both shifts. I wasn't able to visit the South Carolina plant within my month-long time frame, so I called the plant manager and asked him to tell me about every person that worked for him.

On the 30th day, I once again sat at the conference room table across from the president, and the quiz began:

"Okay, Steve, who is Ken?"

"Ken's my boss and your CFO. He came from Boston and a large financial firm to join you."

"That was an easy one. Who are Ron and Sam?"

"Ron is your plant manager at Homeward Way, and Sam is his assistant manager. Ron started with you right out of college as a designer, and you moved him into management. Sam runs our paint shop and has been with you since you started the company. He was one of your first employees."

"Not bad. Let's see if you really know the men. Who's Carl?"

"Carl?" He thought he had me. "Carl works the brake press on second shift. He's a little aloof. Did you know he catches mice at night and then puts them in the press?"

"WHAT??!!"

"Yeah, I thought it was a bit creepy and told him to stop doing it because it was a safety concern. Carl appreciated someone talking to him because he's left on his own most of the time."

And so it continued for almost two hours. The president asked me about people who were in leadership roles as well as those hired in our most remote plant within the past month. I never thought the meeting was going to end. The president finally looked up from his roster and said, "Steve, do you know why you work here now?"

I hesitated to answer because I thought I had made a mistake and was about to lose my job. He said, "You did great and got everyone right. You need to remember one thing —You are here for my people. If you **EVER** forget that, I don't need you."

He didn't scream this. In fact, he was very subdued. He wanted his message to sink deeply and become my philosophy as well. His employees mattered to him, and he expected his human resource person to embody that and value it as much as he did. This sentiment was never put on a wall in a beautiful frame or meant to serve as the introduction to the employee handbook. His philosophy was a reality that was to be lived, understood, and acted on.

I have never forgotten my first assignment in HR. It was daunting when I think about it even to this day. It also serves as an essential foundation for HR in its purest form. The majority of HR practitioners would not do well on this type of assignment because we have lost the focus that people matter and are the reason we even exist. We keep throwing out the catch phrase and "battle cry" to "Put the 'H' back in HR!!" To be honest, this rings hollow and smacks of some Herculean effort to be with people. Putting people first either comes naturally to you as an HR practitioner, or it's something you need to work on. In the end, my president made it crystal clear. If I didn't put people first, I wasn't needed.

Where's your focus??

CHAPTER 3

VERSUS: CHOOSE A SIDE

I AM FORTUNATE to be the father of two incredible kids!! They are actually young adults now, but they will always be my "kids." When my wife and I became parents, we were not given a manual on how to do things right. We were thrown into the middle of new challenges and opportunities every day. We never were given training. In fact, our parents took great pride in seeing us learn on-the-job as our kids grew up. One thing we noticed was that as our kids grew older, they expected my wife and me to take sides. Inevitably, they expected that we would take THEIR side and not the side of their sibling. If my wife or I made the wrong choice, in the eyes of our kids, we'd hear (in an incredibly ear-piercing whine), "That's not fair!!"

I have a question for you: Do you know what happens when kids grow up?

When I've asked this at conferences and at forums, people have bombarded me with answers that were unfortunately negative. We often look down on those who are younger than we are. Hang onto that thought because we'll cover it later. Here's the answer to the question:

They become our employees!!

The same expectation kids have with their parents is what we face in the workplace. The added challenge to this expectation is that now everyone we come into contact with expects us to take his or her side. Managers perceive that HR would automatically support them because they're management. Employees want our support as well. Don't believe the myth that employees feel we support them first. If you asked them, the majority would think that HR supports management before them.

Employees at all levels of an organization expect that all situations involving people should be black and white with no room for anything other than a decision that can never waver. This is unrealistic. We have choices that we need to make every day in HR. Rarely, if ever, are those choices clear-cut absolutes. In practice, though, we come across as if HR is better only if it works from absolutes.

Don't believe me? Let's take a look at an area of our work that we reference probably more than any other—policies and procedures.

We love to create manuals don't we? We get a false sense of comfort that we're controlling the work environment and the performance of others by having more and more policies and procedures. This myth was ingrained in us in childhood as the most effective approach. In school you were expected to stand in lines before being released to an activity. You were not allowed to talk unless you raised your hand and were called on. Everything ran on a schedule with a start time and a stop time. Homework was a daily occurrence, and there were deadlines for projects and exams. If a pop quiz occurred, we were completely thrown because the pattern of our lives was altered.

With that being our background, it's no wonder we want to replicate that environment of structure in our workplaces. The reality of the workplace (and honestly in schools) is that it is a dynamic, ever-changing entity that can accept some forms of structure, but not absolutes. One of two things will take place if you persist in remaining steadfast on policies and procedures as your guiding standard: (a) People won't follow them because you expect the "rule" to be self-explanatory, meaning you see no need to explain the reason for the rule, or (b) you won't follow the policies and procedures in HR, or as supervisors, because you'll make exceptions. Making exceptions is natural because we want to do the right thing when it comes to working with people, so we'll bend the policy to someone's advantage if we enjoy working with the person, and we'll use it as a weapon if we don't.

(Cue the HR purists: We **NEVER** do that!! We treat all of our employees the same because we believe in being fair!!)

I mentioned my kids earlier. One day I was home when they both returned from school. We usually had a snack when they came home, and my daughter walked into the kitchen eyeing an open bag of Oreos. She reached inside the bag to find two cookies left. Her younger brother was tagging along and exclaimed, "I want a cookie too!!"

Now, next to the open bag of Oreos was an unopened bag of Chips Ahoy! chocolate chip cookies. My daughter pulled the two delicious cream-filled Oreos apart, looked directly at her brother, and licked them all over before she popped them into her mouth. He screamed as if she'd slammed his hand in between a door:

"THAT'S NOT FAIR!!!!"

Seeing this as a teachable moment, I said to my son, "What's the problem? You said you wanted a cookie, and we have a whole bag of chocolate chip cookies right here. You said you wanted a cookie."

Not to be outmaneuvered, he said, "But I wanted an Oreo!"

You see, "fair" is defined by the individual and not some system. Fairness is elusive because you can't predict where people are coming from. You can, however, be consistent. Consistency is a much better place to work from because it allows you to take into consideration the situation and the people involved and then find something to address what you're facing.

It's time to make a choice. Are you going to be an HR practitioner who chooses people over processes, or will you remain a traditionalist who chooses processes over people? Please don't think that either side of this choice exists without the other. We tend to put things into components and camps, which sets the stage for conflict. Choosing people first allows you to meet people emotionally and become aware of their passions, perspectives, and motivations. This is critical. If you jump straight to logic and reasoning without first listening to what they have to say about the situation, you'll make a bad decision every time.

I'd like you to try something new in how you view policies and procedures.

Treat them as parameters that you set up that allow people to perform versus as an established set of rules. Open the field for employees to roam, explore, and create. It's what they want, but they don't know how to express it. The reality of the company norms of rules and regulations is inhibiting to most, and they've seen what happens to people who choose to buck the system.

Processes are important, but they need to be road maps that give people definition and direction. If you review your current HR systems, you'll see that they've been set up to force people to comply to set standards. At the same time, you have performance management systems that want to reward people for what they bring to their role and the organization in an innovative and fresh way. Systems of confinement cannot exist with environments of innovation.

I think you'd enjoy your role in HR if you took the time to stop the systems you currently use and evaluate what they *really* do. After your review, compare that with what you'd like the workplace environment to be. See if they line up with each other. If they don't (and I'm pretty sure they won't), then do something different and change your point of view. Put people first!!

CHAPTER 4

ASK ME WHY

EVERYONE KNOWS that the first word that kids master after learning the obligatory "Mama" and "Dada" is "no!!" The one that comes in a close second is "why??" Isn't that great? The first word is all about defiance and defining boundaries. Parents get exasperated because "no" is used so often that when "why" comes along, they feel it's defiant as well. However, when kids ask "why," they're trying to learn and seek context.

This is no different with employees. Some will ask "why" directly, while most will push back either through behavior or nonverbal responses. People want context, which is an incredibly healthy desire. However, HR and management are still stuck in feeling that employees are being defiant. How can we change this attitude? Like most things, change has to start with ourselves. Let's take a look at our current environment.

I love it when people call themselves "change agents." The moment I see this, my first instinct is to test it out. When change agents are faced with a clear opportunity to change, they balk. Every. Time.

The truth is that very few people are comfortable with change—even in the slightest way. We want stability, consistency, and comfort in our daily patterns. This is especially true in the workplace. If you don't think this is true, look at the parking lot outside your office. I guarantee that people park in the same place every day even if they aren't designated a certain spot. If someone dares enter his or her sacred space, stand out in the hall to hear how that employee reacts. You would have thought that the offending parker had mortally wounded the person because he or she took "their" space. This slight alteration in a person's daily pattern could ruin the person's entire day. The employee won't be able to shake the ill will he or she feels toward the person who upset the pattern.

HR professionals fall into one of two camps when it comes to organizational change. They follow either the flavor-of-the-month/best-practice mimicry model or the change-things-as-little-as-possible model. You may find folks who move along a continuum between these two models, but most are entrenched on one side or the other regarding how HR is practiced.

You also have to look at HR from two vantage points—an organization's culture and its view about employees. The word, and behavior, I see most often, is **conformity**. There is so much written about having open work environments, which would allow for innovation and free expression, but they don't exist because the reality is that we want people to fall in line. Now, put this behavior up against the message of change. They don't jive. We can't expect everyone to be the same and open to unique individuality of performance and thought at the same time.

Time for some context about HR.

(Author's note: The next set of questions don't have a right or wrong answer, but they will challenge you to think about your role in and approach to human resources.)

- Have you sat back and wondered why you're in HR?

- Is it something you chose or something you fell into?

- How do you personally feel about human resources?

- How do your company and senior management view the function of human resources?

- Are you geeked in your role in HR or exhausted?

- What is the reason **WHY** you're in HR?

If you can't answer the "why" of this set of questions, you need to reevaluate if human resources is the field for you. Existence just for existence's sake isn't good for you, others, or your company. How can you expect employees to bring their best to work if you don't? Whenever I've asked peers to step back and be reflective about the purpose of why they're in HR, you can see them start to twitch. I don't think many professionals examine why they do what they do. We are all taught that we must work and hold a job, so we do it. It is wonderful that a job can provide an income and a standard of living, but isn't there something more than that?

People thrive when they have a purpose. If this is something you can adopt yourself in HR, you will see a transformation in how you practice your craft. You will also see a marked difference in your approach to, attitude toward, and perspective of your company and your employees.

If we take the position of merely existing in our role, then the people around us will model the behavior we exhibit. To truly change your take on work and the expectations of others with whom you work, print out this sentence and put it on your wall as a reminder, and don't waver from it—ever:

MODEL THE BEHAVIOR YOU EXPECT IN OTHERS!!

Instead of telling people what to do and how to behave, *show* them. This works. It is much easier for people to follow the behavior they see in you versus trying to comply with a set of rules and regulations that are never consistently followed. Wouldn't you enjoy an HR role in which you didn't feel you were constantly chasing others down? Wouldn't it be better if you spent your time on the positive aspects of your people instead of how you're currently practicing HR?

The great thing about modeling your behavior is that you don't need someone's permission or approval from senior management. We continue to be silently cordoned off in organizations by some invisible force field that we feel senior management holds over us. Trust me, if HR sets the example of what great organizational behavior is, senior management will not only jump on board, but its members will give you visible support in what you're doing.

It's time to quit yearning for some place in corporate Valhalla and own who you are and why you're in HR. By taking this initial step, the rest of the world of human resources will open up to you like never before. You can exist fully at any level within an organization from an entry-level HR assistant to a chief human resource officer (CHRO).

The first step is yours.

CHAPTER 5

LAVA LAMPS, MUSIC, AND TOYS

SEVERAL YEARS AGO, an HR friend invited me to visit him at his company. He was the head of recruiting for a national company that makes uniforms (and provides other great services.) I was geeked to get a look behind the scenes of this well-respected company. I knew I had crossed into another organizational dimension than I was used to when I pulled my car into the company's "campus." Its footprint was enormous, and I felt out of place even before I walked into the ornate building.

The minute I entered the lobby, the identically dressed duo of receptionists gazed straight through me. They wore matching red blazers over perfectly pressed white blouses, and each wore a blue scarf around her neck. Before I approached them, I scanned the people milling about the massive edifice, and noticed every single person wore a crisp white shirt with a striped tie or a business suit. As I looked down at my bright yellow golf shirt with khakis, I noted that I was easily identified as an outsider.

The receptionist "twins" were welcoming to a point. I had to make sure to sign in and note my reason for visiting and whom I was scheduled to see. They then pulled out the appropriately colored visitor name badge and asked me to wait until my friend came out of some unseen catacomb to take me into the inner workings of this behemoth. When we made it to his office, I told him how uncomfortable I felt because I didn't look like the other people around me. He then reminded me that I was at a uniform company. The employees were wearing the products the company sold. It all made sense after that.

I walked into their culture. It was obvious that they owned this look and approach, and if you were an employee with this company, you had better buy in as well. It was required.

The concept of "culture" is nothing earth-shattering or new other than the reality of companies now understanding the power of what a culture is and the pressure to conform to its norms. HR has been a steward of culture forever, but usually as an outsider that facilitates contrived, forced social events. It's time to peel back the layers of what culture is and how it affects employees and to understand HR's opportunity within this vast facet of organizational life.

So, just what is culture? A formal definition of it is:

"The totality of socially transmitted behavior patterns, arts, beliefs, institutions, and all other products of human work and thought." (*The American Heritage Dictionary of the English Language*)

An alternative definition is:

"Culture is the number one reason employees stay or leave your company." (Steve Browne, HR savant)

You may be asking, "How is THAT a definition of culture?" It's based on having over three decades of HR experience. If employees leave because you have an awful manager/supervisor, it's because your company's culture allows that person to be awful. If people stay/leave because of your compensation structure, it's reflective of how your company has decided it will pay people. You can take every aspect of how your company works and tie it to culture.

There are a few key elements that you need to review and redirect when it comes to culture.

No. 1. Culture Is Never the Same

Too often companies, and especially HR, take culture and try to mash it into a one-size-fits-all model. We create programs, slogans, posters, and kitschy T-shirts and apparel to communicate these efforts and ensure that we get buy-in from the staff. It never works. Companies pour an incredible amount of energy, focus, and resources into these endeavors, but they quickly become the next flavor of the month or best practice that falls flat and doesn't take hold.

People are not the same. Every single person is unique and brings his or her own mix of skills, strengths, and attributes to the job and to the company. So, if everyone is unique, why do we continue to force conformity or a homogeneous workforce?

No. 2. There Are Many, Many, Many Cultures in Your Company

We have taken the term "culture" to try and describe all attributes of our company. That's not realistic. You have an overall company culture as well as microcultures within departments, locations, geographies, etc. This is a challenge only if you try to shape and make everything fit into a tight package. You need to understand that the more you try to force people into a small box, someone will jump out and do something different. The reason is not that the person is being rebellious; it's simply human nature to explore new boundaries.

No. 3. Senior Management Doesn't Own Culture; HR Does

This is an area of discussion and disagreement in the business world. It is absolutely true that your company's senior management strongly influences business decisions and the environment in the organization. Traditionally, senior management has owned culture by default. The only reason for this is that no one ever pays attention to culture until economic challenges or other problems arise. The first response to these types of pressures is to convene a culture committee or a strategic culture initiative (see point No. 1), and the downward spiral continues to deepen significantly HR hasn't traditionally stepped up to take the reins of culture, but it should. Why is that true? You need to look at an HR math formula:

Culture = people.

People = HR.

Therefore, HR = culture!!

It may seem a bit radical for us to own culture, but every organization needs HR to take responsibility for it. Senior management is looking for HR to step up and take responsibility for guiding culture. HR is in the best position to make this come to life because they are in charge of the people practices of the organization.

Remember the uniform company? Let me share a different environment, and then you can make the comparison between the two.

My office is a menagerie. When you enter it, you encounter an endless number of colors, sounds, and toys. Yes, toys. I also have three lava lamps sitting on a small, wooden file cabinet, and they run constantly. There is one that is an "original" lamp from the '70s with purple globs floating aimlessly up and down. Next to it is one from my kids that is tie-dyed, and the lava changes colors as it moves—very cool. The newest addition was a gift from a fellow HR friend that is a Jedi light saber!!

Placed in front of the lava lamps are a traditional Magic 8 Ball and an Affirmation Ball, which has a smiley face and gives only positive answers. It's the antithesis of the Magic 8 Ball and gives them a bit of positive karma. Off to the left is one of two chairs in my office and hanging precipitously above it is a sword. A real sword (in a sheath). It's fabulous because I require all team members who visit me to sit below it. On my desk you'll find a jelly bean dispenser, various tchotchkes that you can play with, and a mix of books you can borrow and read. My walls are filled with art that doesn't match, including a framed sofa-size print showing the legends of rock 'n' roll music. (I ask people to guess the artists to see how many they know.) Finally, you will **ALWAYS** hear music in my office. I never turn it off regardless of who comes to visit.

Recently, the founder of our company popped in just to say hi. He's an incredible person and a true icon in our community. He looked around my office taking in the mayhem and different items. He stood there for a few minutes without saying anything. I began to get a bit skittish about what he was going to say. I thought I may even get chastised for what he saw.

He took a deep breath and said, "Brownie, I love your office."

I relaxed just a bit, and he continued. "Do you know why I love it?"

"No sir, I don't."

"I love it because it describes what you do for us. Don't change that."

Did you catch that? He feels that my office describes what I do for the company. My office reflects who I am and what I bring to the company and its culture. Is there any bigger endorsement you can get than from the founder of the company?

You have that chance to mold and define the culture of your organization. Culture starts with you. If you approach HR from the hard side of things surrounded by rules and compliance, take a look at your culture and see how much people reflect that. If your approach is intentional, inviting, inquisitive, and intriguing, look at the people around you and see how much they reflect that!!

Remember that there is no "right" or "wrong" culture. HR spends too much time and effort mimicking and copying the companies that are known for their culture. You need to come to grips that your company won't be Google, Southwest Airlines, Starbucks, or Zappos, unless you work there. Make your culture *your* culture. That's a great thing!! The idiosyncrasies and nuances of your company make it what it is. **Own it. Build it. Love it.**

CHAPTER 6

BOTTOM-SHELF THINKING

HR HAS BECOME TOO COMPLEX. It never seems to simplify. It only seems to grow more and more cumbersome for us and our employees. We don't even see it. We rarely evaluate whether a process, procedure, program, or policy is necessary. Once it is published, it turns to granite, and we may tweak it every so often, but it rarely moves.

Add to that the trap of HRspeak and corporatespeak. You know what these are. They mean throwing out corporate catch phrases and pretending that we're communicating with each other. Something like, "So is everyone on the same page? We want to make sure everyone's a team player who's on board so we can create synergy across the department. We'll verify this with analytics, big data, and **SMART** goals."

HR chimes in and launches an onslaught of semilegal terms and endless acronyms like, "I don't think the team understands the implications of the ACA on the FLSA, ADA, ADEA, and FMLA. We don't want the DOL coming in unexpectedly on this, and if we don't have forms 1094, 5500, and 1095c in line, I'd hate to see what happens!!" And on and on it goes.

You may talk this way when you're in a meeting with other departments or senior management to seem to fit in. I promise that internally you're hoping you don't get asked what any of that HRspeak means because you probably can't explain it. It's a sickening feeling because you want to be included in the organization, but this form of language never feels natural. It internally makes you shiver when you either hear it or feel forced into using it.

The reality is that no one **REALLY** talks this way. Authors of books and blogs use these buzzwords because it gives them incredible latitude to come up with a 5-, 7- or 10-step miracle plan that will work in solving your HR challenges. There are no simple remedies in HR. There never have been. The reason is that something always gets in the way—people.

Have you ever been in a meeting when people throw these types of terms around, and everyone nods in approval, but no one ever asks for clarity? You go out in the hall outside the conference room where the meeting just happened, and then the **REAL** meeting starts!! This isn't wrong; it's a reality. In these hallway conversations, things get broken down into terms and language that are more tangible and realistic. You feel better because this is what you wanted to talk about in the meeting but didn't know how to do it. The pressure to conform in those settings is so great that you're not willing to break the norms.

What if you could take the great approach, tone, and conversations that happen in the "meeting after the meeting" and make those the norm? It's possible, but you have to trust that a shift in your approach will take hold. This leap may feel huge, but this approach is actually more natural for us. We just have lost sight of how to practice it.

Take everything you do and put it on the bottom shelf.

When you go into a grocery store, you are drawn to the things placed to catch your eye. Companies intentionally pay for better shelf space so that you will look at their brands in the hope that you're more likely to buy their goods.

We have to do this in HR. We have to get in the line of sight of our employees and make our goods attractive and accessible. There is a "cost" to doing this, and you must know that going into this. Companies don't want things on the bottom shelf. The approach poses a threat because it seems so odd and unlike any practice that regularly occurs.

Let me tell you a story ...

Several years ago I started at a job as a company's first dedicated HR person. One of the executives had been handling HR, along with her other duties, for years, but the company had grown considerably, and management felt it was time for a dedicated human resource practitioner. My first day of work, I dressed up more than usual because I wanted to make a good first impression. I even wore a tie!! (This is not the norm for me. You have to know that.) After the obligatory introductions to all the staff and a tour of the offices, I settled down in my own office. My boss, the executive who had been handling HR, asked me to take a look at the employee handbook as my first project because it hadn't been updated in years.

I was eager, and I wanted to see what kind of culture I had just entered. Did I mention that I was working for engineers and architects? I cracked open the spine of the handbook and started to read. It was in classic handbook style, format, and flow. Someone had used a handbook template, because every policy had a title, purpose, and then endless minutia that did nothing and was ignored by any employee who took the time to actually read the handbook. It was a phenomenal example of a command and control document with endless layers of redundancy. In fact, being an engineering firm, EVERY policy was numbered—1.0, 1.1, 1.1a, 1.1b, 1.1c, 1.2, etc. It was mind-boggling to witness and impossible to understand. **EVERY** policy!!

After suffering through the eight-page policy on making coffee (true story for another time), I found something that caught my eye: the dress code. I hate dress codes. They're inane and unnecessary. If you have a need for certain clothing to perform your job, then fine. Other than that, they shouldn't exist. It's another example of a rule set for us to closely confine people that has nothing to do with their performance. But I digress ...

I took this job in the late 1990s when "business casual" was just starting to become part of a company's vocabulary. We were still heavily in the days of suits regardless of the industry. The handbook I was reading said that the dress code at the firm was business casual, but the only employee without a suit coat (including the women) was me. I had the audacity to wear a tie but no coat on my first day!! Rebel.

I decided that day to push the norms and put something on the bottom shelf. On my second day, I wore a shirt and slacks with no tie or coat. You'd think I'd learn like a good HR person to fit in and conform. Better to keep things status quo than rock the boat. Nope—not me at all.

I didn't parade around or call myself out to anyone. I went to my office and began to work. My office was located near the C-suite's offices, even though I wasn't there yet. I came in early, and the CEO had to walk past my office to reach his. He came by and saw me, and I waved good morning. He stopped in front of my office and turned bright red. He scurried down the hall and slammed the door to his office. My boss sat directly across from me, and her phone started instantly ringing. I could hear the CEO screaming through her phone for five minutes. She kept calm and said she would address it.

After she hung up, she walked over to me and asked me where my tie was. I said that I was following policy and didn't wear one. She looked puzzled and asked which policy I was following. I explained to her that we stated we had a "business casual" environment, and I interpreted that as not having to wear a tie. I assured her that I was in compliance with the policy with the rest of my attire. She smirked and understood. She even giggled a bit. She said, "You remind me of someone who came here years ago and made some changes that were needed." She walked down to the CEO's office, knocked, and went in. Twenty minutes later she came out and winked at me.

The CEO never talked to me the rest of that day. I wondered if it was going to be my last. It wasn't. The third day of my employment I again went to work without tie. I took my position at my desk, and then he walked by. The CEO passed by my office, waved, and smiled. No tie.

The rest of the office wondered if we were going to have layoffs because the CEO wasn't wearing a tie or coat. They couldn't believe what was going on, and several of them asked me what happened.

I said that he was following policy and told them that we were allowed to dress business casual. I didn't embellish on how the CEO had lost his mind the day before. I just told them that it was okay to be casual. The fourth day in the office only two or three men wore ties. The culture changed because I read the handbook.

Afterward, I dismantled the entire document and put it in language that was conversational and understandable. I took out all the numbers and purposes and laid out the framework of what we expected so that people could do their jobs. Oh, the eight-page coffee policy disappeared too.

What are the things in your organization that need to be moved to the bottom shelf? I would wager that you could find several examples of things that should be reevaluated, stripped down, and simplified. Putting things in the reach of your employees is a subtle effort and not a vaunted program. You need to ask yourself, "Are we doing things that hinder our ability for our people to perform?" If the answer is "yes," then address it. Don't let it continue to be in the way.

Communicate with people directly and honestly. Drop the HRspeak and corporatespeak and talk to each other as humans. Do it in every communication that comes from HR. Don't compromise ever. You can break down years of sludge and open new avenues for people to actually talk to each other.

When you do this (not *if*, but *when*), you will see a company transform itself. It can occur only if you take the first step. This isn't someone else's responsibility—it's yours. Even though there will be doubters and those who want to hold onto the norms that they have so willingly embraced, reach up on the top shelf and move things down.

CHAPTER 7

BE STRATEGIC DAILY

I WAS BROUGHT UP in a family with an amazing work ethic. Most of my extended family came from a farming background where hard work is a fact. I remember staying with my grandparents, aunts, and uncles as a young child. We woke up before dawn and worked straight through until nightfall. Many tasks needed attention every day. There weren't "days off" because we were always paying attention to animals, crops, and equipment. I'm thankful for my experiences on the farms and sometimes yearn for that constant stability!!

I learned that you need to "get your work done." I didn't learn much about planning, forecasting, or brainstorming. The concept of having a broad perspective on work wasn't even on my mind. So when I started in HR as an internal recruiter, I did what I was told (like on the farm). Take the open requisitions I received, source candidates, interview them, extend a job offer, repeat. Even though it was a narrow focus as a job, I enjoyed the consistency. There was a small portion of variety in the roles I filled and the people I met, but my scope was contained, and that worked for me and the organization … for a while.

I had an inkling that human resources had to offer more than what I was experiencing. However, I didn't know how to explore other dimensions of the profession. Making the jump from a specialist role to a generalist role seemed logical, but I had no idea how unprepared I was. HR generalist roles require you to wear somewhere between 10 to 1,000 hats at one time. That is true Every. Single. Day. Variety is the norm, and it isn't always your friend. It's very easy for the pace of a "regular" day to come crashing over you in ways you never anticipated.

When I've met and talked with other HR professionals and asked them what they do, the answer that most people give is, "I put out fires." Before you read on, reread that statement and think about it.

If you only put out fires in HR, then you better change professions so you get to wear the gear. If you're a firefighter in HR, you're being reactionary. Granted, things will come up that you need to address, but if everything is a fire, then something is not going well. Also, if your company hired you only to be a firefighter, you need to question how it views the function of human resources in the first place. You shouldn't be in a position where you sit by a large, red phone just expecting the next emergency to occur.

For the past 15 years, HR has yearned for the mythical "seat at the table." Countless books, magazine articles, blogs, and conference presentations have used this phrase to rally HR professionals forward using this as a battle cry. HR practitioners look at this seat as some crowning achievement that will finally validate who they are and what they do for the organization. The problem is that the seat has already passed us by because we continue to practice transactionally (tasks perspective) versus being strategic (global perspective).

How can we be strategic if we're always fighting fires? The answer is you can't because you are never ahead of your circumstances. The unfortunate reality is that most HR practitioners don't function in a strategic manner. We tend to have people come to us—but the reason is rarely for our input, business insight, or brainstorming about solutions to issues facing the organization. People come to HR to fix problems and put out fires.

When you're in a position in which people view you as someone who is to be engaged only when needed, you'll never be viewed from a strategic vantage point. To be honest, this realization is very disheartening, and I think it's become an almost insurmountable barrier for many HR professionals. Being separate from the organization tends to eat at you, and it's understandable that many throw in the towel.

This doesn't have to be how you are viewed in your company or personally. In fact, you should stand up and push back on how companies have tended to relegate the HR function. One thing has to change for this to occur.

Quit yearning to be seen as strategic. **BE INTENTIONALLY STRATEGIC IN ALL YOU DO!!**

We have to quit thinking that we're in HR. The reality is that we're businesspeople who happen to practice HR. This is true whether you actually approach your role from this perspective or not. We need to understand that senior management wants only people who will perform and move the business forward. Therefore, we have a daily opportunity to be strategic in how we approach our role, our employees, and the situations we tackle.

HR has an advantage over most departments in companies because we work with every department and people at every level. This gives you an incredible landscape and access to work with the C-suite as well as with people on the front line.

You can start being strategic daily through one simple practice—be a connector.

Instead of jumping from person to person and opinion to opinion, step back and see the different components and people who are interacting. Fight your urge to take on these interactions individually. When you step back, you can evaluate and see where connections can occur. Doing this gives a broader perspective, and you won't get buried in minutia. Bringing various people together can do so many positive things. It encourages work across departments and teams. It shows them how they are all interconnected and interdependent like a giant web. The more you can connect people, the more you are acting strategically because you're facilitating different perspectives that should lead to more holistic business solutions.

You will still have fires to address, but acting transactionally doesn't have to be the primary identifier in what you provide to your company. Put the axe, coat, and helmet away, and pick up the clipboard or tablet. Move out into your organization and dive deep into the various departments. Decide today to spend time with people in their environment so you're no longer seen only as the principal's office where people come when they're troubled.

Trust me. When you take the steps to be out among the people, you can't help but be strategic. The company will see this, your frustration will begin to dissipate, and you will be encouraged in who you are and what you do!!

CHAPTER 8

ALL BY MYSELF

DO YOU REMEMBER the '70s song "All by Myself" by Eric Carmen? It wasn't an uplifting song by any means, but it has some haunting lyrics that capture HR at times. Check them out:

"Hard to be sure / Sometimes I feel so insecure ... / All by myself / Don't want to be / All by myself anymore"

It was a giant hit on AM radio. (Note: Radio is how we used to listen to music, but I digress.)

The majority of my career I was by myself in HR. Today we call this an "HR department of one" to make it more acceptable. The majority of small, midsize, and some large companies devote only one position to HR. It can be very daunting because you are responsible for every single facet of human resources, and you don't have the luxury of tapping into any internal folks to help you out. What's intriguing about people who are in this position is that they rarely reach out to find help.

When I was in my first HR generalist role, the company where I needed to remember everyone's name, I struggled to even comprehend what HR meant. I tried to pick up information where I could, but this was long before the advent of the Internet. I didn't know how to connect with other folks in HR. I was about as isolated as I could get.

However, it was an incredible training ground!! I didn't know that at the time, but it was guerrilla HR, meaning learning through experiences. This hasn't changed much. Sure, you can find more resources through the Internet, but the majority of people in departments of one are still isolated. The challenge is that people feel pressure, real or assumed, that they are indispensable, so they don't reach out to other professionals. Granted, the vast majority of HR professionals in departments that have many staff don't reach out to other professionals either.

Why is that, and when did we think this was a good way to approach what we do?

The argument that I've often heard is that since companies don't allocate adequate training dollars, people still feel forced to make it on their own. This survivalist mentality is not healthy, and it often leads to burnout. When HR folks are isolated, they tend to leave the profession and try other careers instead of sticking with it.

I worked in great company cultures as the sole HR professional. Working in a great environment made me feel included as part of the organization even though I didn't have anyone to bounce HR ideas off of. Don't get me wrong, I worked with people at all levels of the company, but I was honestly guessing at what to do. I encountered very few obstacles that couldn't be solved when I was on my own. Even so, I just know now that I would have benefited from having others around who could understand what practicing HR entails.

One of the biggest challenges we face as HR professionals is that we have no one to talk to inside our organizations. This isn't because we're unfriendly. It's just because we deal with situations and information that can't be shared. The reality of confidentiality is a daily weight. It tends to only grow, and that can be overwhelming. I know there were many times when I felt I would just burst. If I had to handle one more investigation or learn the facts behind a difficult or awkward employee situation, I thought I'd break down. I wanted to turn to someone to help cope with this pressure, but there was no one in the organization that I could go to. It's an awful feeling to be surrounded by employees and still feel completely alone.

To meet people in my field, I got involved in HR-related groups, such as my local HR chapter (I'll cover this later in the book). Talking with others who could relate to being a department of one helped me. However, I didn't feel truly connected. Most of the people I met were fantastic humans, but most remained acquaintances whom I saw every so often. I sensed I needed something else that would anchor me more.

And then something unexpected occurred that saved me. Literally. I met Fred.

Fred was a seasoned HR professional who started practicing when the field was called "personnel" and men held most of the positions. Personnel was more labor oriented and primarily had an administrative and compliance focus. We met while volunteering for the Ohio State Council of the Society for Human Resource Management (SHRM). He was very welcoming and friendly. Only later did I realize that we both lived and worked in the same area of the state. He reached out after we met and started to regularly check in with me. We talked about everything when it came to HR. He did more listening than talking when we were first getting to know each other. Over time, I listened to Fred often and sought his advice on situations on a more regular basis. He was patient, interested, genuine, and wise. He also was safe to talk to, and he allowed me to vent. When someone takes the time to be present just because you need him or her to be available for you—that's the mark of a true friend.

I had no idea that he was my mentor. I never looked at him that way until I stepped back and reflected on our relationship. He was such a great mentor that the relationship was seamless and not forced into existence. He showed interest in me and then stuck with it. After some time, I realized that Fred silently mentored several people. I was very fortunate to have him step into my career at the time he did. He shared a passion for people and for HR. This was what I needed. HR stayed wonderful, and he showed me how to be a better HR practitioner.

Fred continues to be my mentor, and we're going on well over 15 years now. When I had a chance, I nominated him for Mentor of the Year in our local HR chapter, and he was chosen. The audience members rose to their feet when he won because he had positively influenced so many lives.

Fred introduced me to a broader HR community, including those professionals he considers mentors to him. He changed my entire thinking about mentorship. Through his experience and actions, he taught me the **power of three:**

You can't be a mentor to another unless you have a mentor yourself.

Because I've had Fred as my mentor, I have developed the confidence to mentor others.

If you are a self-proclaimed mentor, then you really just want people to bow to your wisdom and knowledge. It's a very selfish perspective. You see, I didn't mention that Fred introduced me to a much broader HR community, including those professionals he considered mentors to him. He was the one who taught me the power of three by his actions and example.

If you're in that department-of-one situation, you need to get a mentor in your life as well as reach out to and mentor someone else. Connect with other HR professionals who are also departments of one. You have so much in common, and knowing that you're there for each other will give you the encouragement, the release, and the anchor you need.

Although some mentorships last only a year, I feel that kind of relationship is more like coaching than mentoring. The type of mentor I'm talking about is there for you in the long term as a friend, a peer, a resource, and an outlet. Your relationship with your mentor should be beneficial for both of you. I never would be the person or HR professional I am without Fred. That's a fact, and he taught me that I was never by myself.

You need to understand that if you practice HR in isolation, you will either reach a point of burnout or you'll walk away from the field. We can't succeed by ourselves. You may be able to do this for a time, but you will succumb in the end. Why would you want that to be your future as an HR professional?

You may think that you can't be a mentor. You may even think you don't have enough of value to offer another person. Those doubts just aren't true. It's negative language that keeps you from moving forward and connecting with others. You see, when Fred stepped forward, he made himself available. That was it. That was the first step. He didn't have a schedule or a plan of how things would develop. We let our mentoring relationship grow naturally. When you allow yourself to be available, you never know what will occur. That may be a bit overwhelming because the unknown usually is. However, it's a step worth taking.

Make yourself available. Find a mentor and then be a mentor. When you do this, you will see your experience in HR blossom.

CHAPTER 9

WHERE IS HE?

ONE OF THE PAST HR JOBS I held in manufacturing taught me an incredible lesson. I was the company's first person hired dedicated to human resources. I had held that role before, and I welcomed the opportunity to bring the HR function to life. This company was unique because it made nuts and bolts—literally. It was a fastener company with a predominantly blue-collar environment with a small sales staff and an administrative staff.

During my first week, I was out on the floor talking to the employees while they worked to get to know them. Little did I know that while I was out on the floor, the founder and owner of the tool and die company, Ken, was in the office. He was nearing retirement, so he came in a few days a week. My office and his were along the same hall with his being a larger corner office and mine a functional office right off the front door. Ken was known to take a walk through the office each time he came into work. He knew I had been hired and had started this week, and when he walked past my office, he stopped, confused. (I later heard this from his administrative assistant who was watching him and was intrigued to see what would happen.) Ken evidently stopped his rounds, walked down the hallway back toward his office and into the office of my new boss, Walt, the CFO.

"Where is he?" asked Ken.

"Where is who?" replied Walt.

"The new HR guy. I went by his office, and he wasn't there. Did he come in today?" asked Ken.

"I'm sure he's here, Ken," answered Walt nervously.

"Well, if he ever decides to come back to his desk, tell him I want to see him!" demanded Ken.

"Yes, sir," Walt said sheepishly.

Ken returned to his corner executive office, and my boss left his office on the hunt for me. I was just finishing my rounds on the floor, and he met me at the double doors as I came out of the plant and walked toward my desk.

"Where were you, Steve?" Walt said in a forced, angry tone.

I was a bit struck by this and said, "I was out on the floor like I have been every day."

"Ken was looking for you. And he wants to see your right now!" insisted Walt.

I didn't understand why there was such a sense of urgency, but I walked around the interior cube farm past Walt's office and knocked on Ken's door.

"You wanted to see me, sir?" I asked.

"Steve, I came by your desk this morning, and you weren't there. What were you up to?" asked Ken.

"I was out on the floor talking to the employees. I do it every day at the beginning of each shift," I replied.

"Why in the world would you do that?" Ken wondered.

"It's a great way to see how everyone is doing, and I get to make sure that someone says 'good morning' or 'good afternoon.' It's just a simple way to check in and let them know we appreciate them being at work," I said.

"Do you think this is an effective use of your time?" Ken asked sarcastically.

"Yes sir, I do. I get more of a pulse of how everyone's doing by meeting with them, and I think it's important to make those connections. You can hear about things sooner before they become a problem. I did this in my prior job in another manufacturing company, and it really helped our employee relations."

"So, how are the men?" I could tell he was testing me because he didn't think I should be on the floor. I had to be hindering production, and why in the world would the HR guy be with the people on the front line?

I looked right at him and said, "Not too good, to be honest. They have several concerns, and it seems that people aren't listening to them. I've only been here a few days, but some of the items they are talking about should be reviewed and addressed. I'm just listening right now to get to know them."

Ken turned 18 shades of red and stood up. "We'll just see how the men are!! Come with me."

He stormed out of the offices up front and walked with purpose out to Don who ran a Landis. A Landis threads bolts of steel, and there are four heads on the machine. Don would feed the heads from right to left, and by the time he got the fourth bolt loaded, he reached back to the first head and flipped the bolt over so the other end could be threaded as well. It was a leaky, old, and junky machine, and Don was literally covered from head to toe in machine grease. He did this job every day and was one of the company's most tenured machinists.

Ken abruptly came up to Don and loudly said, "Don! How are you doing?"

Don became ghostly pale, dropped some pieces that were supposed to be threaded, and mumbled, "I'm fine, sir. Thanks for asking."

That was the end of the conversation. Ken turned around and beckoned me to come back to his office. When we got there, he forcefully closed his door and told me to take a seat.

"I think the men are fine, Steve," he stated confidently.

"I disagree, Ken."

"What?? You saw that I talked to Don, and he told me he was doing fine," he replied defiantly.

"That's just one person, sir. Did you know that I was out talking to Don just this morning about his bad attitude and his ongoing attendance problem? Also, I was talking to him because your plant manager, Carl, is fed up and said he just can't get through to Don, but he doesn't want to fire him because no one else wants to work on the Landis that just belches and leaks more and more each day. Carl has asked maintenance to fix it, but your VP of operations won't approve the expense to repair it. Don is critical because he makes one of our base products, and we don't think that we can have the machine go down too long, so we just limp along."

"How long have you worked here, Steve?"

"Three days, sir."

"And you already know all this, how?"

"I told you. I go out and visit the employees to see what they're doing and listen to them."

"Well, I'll be darned. I have people who have been here for years who wouldn't have the courage to tell me what you just did. In fact, I pay some of them very well to be straight with me. You keep visiting the employees. It's a bit odd to me, but I like what I hear."

"Thank you, sir," and I went back down to my office. This is when the story gets **REALLY** good!!

Ken left his office and walked next door to Walt and recounted our conversation and how I stood up to him. He was tickled that I did and congratulated Walt on finding a good HR person who seemed like he was already fitting in. Walt smiled and thanked Ken for the feedback.

What do you think happened next? Let me give you a clue. It should have included some ominous music as Walt walked down to my office and softly closed the door.

"WHO THE HELL DO YOU THINK YOU ARE?" screamed Walt.

"I'm sorry? Is there something wrong?"

"How dare you talk to the founder that way!! If you keep this up, you won't last here long. You can guarantee that!!"

I couldn't let this pass. "Wait, Walt. You're mad at me because I was honest with Ken. Is that it?"

"Just watch yourself," he said, and he stormed out of my office. Remember, that was my third day on the job.

I stayed in that role a little over two years. Oh yes, I still went out on the floor every day to see the employees at the beginning of each shift. It wasn't long before I had strong relationships built with everyone on the manufacturing side even though senior leaders didn't like that I chose this focus. They felt that I should be focusing on them instead of on the employees.

We talk today about generational differences as if they're a new aspect of the workplace. Generational stereotypes have plagued the workplace ever since workplaces have existed. At this company, the myth of being "visible" implied that you were working. So employees who worked in the office stayed out of the plant because they didn't want senior management to see an empty desk. This was, and still is, viciously shortsighted. Being seen doesn't ensure that people are being productive in any way whatsoever.

HR has been chained to its desk for generations. Most of this is by choice as well as how senior management has viewed the contributions of HR. The sad part is that HR practitioners rarely fight against this expectation. We have been lulled into a mode of hibernation that has kept us separated from our employees and, in turn, the organization as a whole.

I want you to adopt a new approach that is honestly overdue:

LEAVE YOUR DESK!! IT WON'T MISS YOU WHILE YOU'RE GONE!!

There has been this ongoing cute phrase to put the "H" back into HR as a way to make sure we keep "humans" in HR. That is crud.

If we are at a point where we need to be reminded to be more human in what we do, then we have serious issues. A catch phrase or a motivational poster on the wall won't ever change behavior. Action will. Get out from behind your desk and your computer, and put away your phone. Make time each day to have genuine "face time" with the humans in your organization. Don't even try to use the size of your company as an excuse either. There are countless ways to get in front of people you work with and spend time with them.

If your senior leadership team thinks that spending time with employees "just because" is a waste of your time, then leave that company. I guarantee that HR will never have a prominent place within that type of culture because the people are more inconvenient than valued.

I know that you want to make HR matter to yourself personally and to your organization. It starts with you taking the step to break the norms and barriers that exist all around you. Be with your people. They're longing for someone to see them, listen to them, and pay attention. Trust me when I tell you that as soon as you stop using your desk to confine you and let it just hold papers like it's supposed to, then HR will become worth doing.

CHAPTER 10

DEALING WITH THE DARK SIDE

WORKING WITH PEOPLE IS TOUGH. It's much more challenging than working with processes or procedures because things don't talk back. People are unpredictable, moody, emotional, and driven by so many different motives that you just can't keep up with them. When I see HR people at conferences, I just want to run up to them and give them a hug. I've done this (with the people I know), and they melt and relax in my arms every time. Working with people is tough, and we don't think that others empathize with that or even understand.

You see, if you broke down an HR person into components, you'd find a mix of 60 percent psychologist, 20 percent paralegal, and 20 percent administrator/compliance officer. I think that's a healthy breakdown of components. Some people spend more than 40 percent of their time and effort on the legal and compliance items. This isn't right or wrong, but my contention is that HR people float toward those legal and compliance components more easily because those two areas tend to be more black and white. They are concrete and don't talk back.

All of the so-called "soft side" of HR is consistently avoided because we have the misconception that absolutes will work with people. However, they don't and never have. We need to come to terms with the fact that we swim in an ocean of gray because we work with humans. We have to figure out a way for this not to be overwhelming and a cause for career burnout. If we don't, then we're doomed to continue practicing HR the way it has been practiced for decades.

People are tough. But we've forgotten a key fact in this statement. You see, we're people too!!

We lose sight of the reality that we are probably tough for someone else to deal with as well. Be honest. Have you ever been the person who is difficult, challenging, or whiny? I have, and I'm sure you have as well. However, when we deal with people all the time, we never put ourselves in the mix. This is a mistake, and the minute you take yourself out, you're going to become calloused and bitter. You will continue to see the dark side of others, and that will be your focus and approach to HR in general.

The reality of our role in HR is that we do hear the complaints and concerns of others on a daily basis. I know several HR peers who resent being the company dumping ground. You'd think this would come only from front-line employees, but you can get dumped on from every level of the company, from the CEO to the front lines. HR needs to provide an avenue for people to get things off their chest and be a release. " However, we need to be able to provide this release while trying to avoid the personal drain of constantly wading through the dark side of people's behaviors.

I've found four ways that have helped me address the dark side of HR over my career. These approaches work and have allowed me not only to cope but to work through those times that wanted to swallow me.

1. Remember That *Everyone* Has Value

We always talk about employees as if they aren't people. It's unfortunate, but we do. In an environment where we call people "talent" and we focus on "high potentials," we ignore the vast majority of people. I like the idea that people are talented because it's a fact. When your first thought is that people have innate talent when you interact with them, you'll see the value they truly possess.

We need to move away from the practice of pulling out a manual and dealing with people solely through policies and procedures. You need to address people as people first. If their behavior falls into an area that deserves discipline, then be consistent with it. However, you must meet with the employee first and see what's happening with him or her before launching into a short-sighted action just to lessen the pain.

Each one of us has "stuff" going on in our lives. We can't lose sight of that. When you approach interactions with the intention of understanding first before acting, you'll be surprised how you'll come up with alternative solutions. HR needs to be the benchmark and champion of all employees. I know this sounds utopian, but it is where we add the most value ourselves.

2. Surround Yourself with Positive People

This is more than the usual "be positive" encouragement. If you are around other HR professionals who are as positive as you are, then you have a community that gives you different perspectives to consider. If you continue to swim with people who talk about people only negatively, then you have no hope of being positive yourself. Being positive is not naturally how we approach life, and it takes an incredible effort to accomplish. I personally find this to be a shame, but it's a reality. I also know that when I've brought this up to others, they get discouraged because they can't think of any positive people off the top of their head. If that is the case with you, then realize that the dark side of HR has become your dominant viewpoint, and it should encourage you even more to change your approach.

Being a positive person is challenging when others are skeptical, and they think it's a show instead of believing that your approach is authentic. That saddens me, but it doesn't sway me. I have been fiercely positive my entire life. Whenever the darkness comes, and it does, I have a stronger base to work from because I have chosen to also build my core group of friends with positive folks. It's a huge step that changes you.

3. Have an Accountability Partner

You will slip and get dark. It's impossible not to have this happen. However, you need to have an anchor or two who will be there for you no matter what. They are your "confessors" to whom you can make your feelings known, and they'll be there for you no matter what you share or feel.

This is different from having a mentor, although a mentor may fill this role for you as well. Accountability is often seen in organizations from a negative perspective. It isn't negative in any way. Having someone by your side who is willing to accept you for who you are, warts and all, is a gift. The idea that you can just tough it out and make it through all situations regardless of how difficult they are is unrealistic. We are better when we have someone in our life who holds us accountable. Many people claim they want "balance" in their lives, but what they really mean is that they want less conflict and stress.

Having an accountability partner will give you the balance you seek because he or she will call out your blind spots or behavior that starts to get cloudy around the edges. Make sure that your accountability relationship is one that allows for give and take, grace, and honest, direct feedback. When you have this kind of relationship in your life, you will be amazed by how much of a tangible and beneficial difference it makes.

4. Be the Light in the Dark

I know this sounds like a catch phrase, but hear me out. You have the choice as to how you will approach people every single day. If you think poorly about others, it will show. If people constantly bring a sigh to you and not a smile, then you can see how they view you.

I get geeked when I see others. It doesn't matter if they're employees or strangers I pass by in a public place. You have the opportunity to positively affect everyone who comes into your life. Something as simple as a "hello" or a brief smile may be just what someone needs to shatter the darkness he or she is dealing with. Never assume that great efforts and initiatives are needed to act. You have the ability to be the light. The decision is yours.

I know that others provide light in my life, and I hope that I am the light in others. It's something that is a very conscious part of how I live each day. I just happen to do it through HR as well.

CHAPTER 11

REMOVING BOULDERS

MOST PEOPLE ARE NEGATIVE. You might be saying, "Duh, who doesn't know that?" It may be apparent that this is how most people view work and life in general, but it still hurts to type it. Seriously, have you ever taken a break from the daily grind and considered this? I want you to try an exercise before you read on:

- Get out a piece of paper (no computers allowed on this one).

- On the left-hand side of the paper, list all the things you are currently working on. Make sure you list everything, not just the large projects.

- Make two columns next to the list of items you're working on— Positive and Negative.

- Then, take a pen or pencil and mark which column your work falls under.

- Note: If you list things like difficult employee situations, compliance for compliance's sake, discipline, and terminations, those get a mark in the Negative column.

- Add up the totals marks in each column, and see which one has more marks.

I'd bet a milkshake that most lists would be more negative in tone. This isn't wrong; it's just a very challenging part of human resources. Think about it. If the majority of your job isn't positive, how difficult is it for you to have a great attitude toward what you do and whom you work with? You have to ask yourself, "If what I do is more negative than positive, why do I put up with it?"

This doesn't have to be the case at all when it comes to great HR. The component missing in how you practice HR is your **approach**. Please note that I'm not casting stones. For many, many years I practiced HR on the negative side of the ledger. I thought the only way I could show value at work was to identify problems, call them out, and then fix them. If this sounds like how you are experiencing HR, you have the chance to step back and pause. Ask yourself this:

Is everything (and everyone) at work really broken?

Negativity breeds negativity. It never does anything constructive, and it only leads to angst, frustration, and ineffectiveness. It's astonishing how little negativity needs to occur for the morale of many people to be squelched. It can literally be as small as one employee who walks around with a gray cloud that always seems to rain on all that the person does. People just cringe at the thought of interacting with that person or even being near him or her. When I hear one my peers say that he or she loves being in HR because he or she is a "people person" who just loves everyone, I giggle. It's just not true. Don't believe me? Time for another pause.

Just for a moment, think of all the people you work with. Can you think of someone who drains you and others? How long did it take for you to think of someone? Less than a second?

Since this is such a strong force to constantly push against, it's no wonder that people in HR become discouraged. You have to wonder if there's a way to destroy the waves of negativity. The great news is that there is a simple way to do this, if you're willing to approach what you do differently.

Each day we have countless opportunities to interact with people and get after problems. Don't get me wrong; solving problems is valuable. The sad thing to me is that "problems" are a small portion of what we actually face each day, and great things are absolutely overlooked. It's all because of the **boulders**.

What are boulders? These are the things that get in the way of people being productive. I know that's a broad definition, but it simplifies work if you think about it. The dilemma we face is that boulders are different for each person and each situation in an organization. They present stumbling blocks that impede people and cause massive frustration. It's hard to identify these boulders if you practice HR in a traditional manner because you are buried in minutia that doesn't allow you to see boulders all around you.

I want to propose a new way for you to practice HR. It's the **SLR** model:

Step back.

Look around.

Remove boulders.

Here's an example: I had a manager in one of my past roles who was very productive and got things done, but few people enjoyed being around him. The majority of his staff kept to themselves versus confronting him, but the mumbling that occurred daily was deafening!! When I talked to his staff and heard that he was not very empathetic, I talked to him about it. He told me that he wasn't hired to make people like him. He was supposed to get stuff done. I didn't fight back, but I kept this in the back of my mind. I had a feeling that it would come up someday and that I'd be in a better place to address his attitude toward others.

What compounded this problem is that the senior leaders of the company knew this manager was a curmudgeon, and they never confronted him about it. He was a producer and had tenure, so no one poked him. That was before I joined the organization.

Do you remember the epic '70s television show "WKRP In Cincinnati"? If you don't, you really need to go find old episodes and check them out. There was a character on the show named Les Nessman who desperately wanted to have a door to his cubicle. He put tape on the floor and was furious if anyone ever entered his space without fake knocking.

Back to my manager. He was in an office that had a sliding glass door. Each morning he was one of the first in the office and diligently at his desk working. As other employees came to work, they silently walked by his office because they knew better than to disturb him. I watched this for several weeks, and then I made my move. I waited until the day was well under way, and then I made my rounds around the office. As I came to this manager's office with his open door, I quietly stepped across the threshold, took a deep breath, and leaned in close to the manager and shouted, **"MORNING, BOB!!!"**

His head snapped up, and his eyes were wide with shock. You could see the veins in his neck start to throb, and he replied through clenched teeth, "What are you doing in my office? You didn't knock!"

"Don't know, just thought I'd drop by and say good morning."

He shot up and stomped down the hallway and went up to my boss's office. He slammed her door and said, "Who does this HR guy think he is?"

"What did Steve do, Bob?"

He stammered, looked down at his feet and said, "He said 'good morning' to me."

"Really? That's awful. I'm sorry he did that."

"You don't understand! He came into my office, didn't knock, and loudly greeted me. He scared me, and I don't appreciate how he did this. What are you going to do about it?"

"Nothing."

"Nothing? What do you mean?"

"Nothing. Bob, you've been dead for years. It's about time that someone breathed some life back into you."

He left my boss's office stunned. This wasn't the response he expected.

Fast forward a few months. I made sure to drop by Bob's office every day to say "good morning." I didn't miss a day, but I never did it loudly again. He stopped me one day and asked me to come in, and we took time to get to know each other. I found out that he was an amazing craftsman who made custom furniture. I had no idea that he was an artist. I asked him if he'd bring in a sample, and he did!! When he brought it in, I asked him if I could take it around to show others. He was a bit embarrassed, but he agreed. I took the piece around the entire office and shared it. When people asked who made it, I told them that Bob did. They were floored.

You see, Bob didn't know that isolating himself from others was a boulder. He had so much to offer but kept to himself. Once he opened up, I found him to be a brilliant person and incredible contributor.

Our job in HR is to step back and get out of the weeds that threaten to swallow us, look around our environment, and spot the boulders. The difference is that we need to step in and remove them. When we do that, we provide incredible value across the entire organization.

CHAPTER 12

HEY, YOU'RE DIFFERENT!!

I MENTIONED EARLIER that negativity is a predominant force in HR. It really is a force that clamps down on the workplace in general, and that is why practicing human resources can be overwhelming. You've probably worked in a variety of environments or industries. Have you ever stood in a hallway, conference room, or break room and just listened? You should really try it, but be prepared to feel slimy.

Most conversations you overhear involve people talking unfavorably about others who are disappointing them. This talk isn't just work related either. People tend to want to gossip and share dirt about situations. It doesn't help that we are constantly surrounded by an endless stream of social media and news feeds that tend to glorify tragedies and fuel our need to feel better than the poor people featured on these forums. One more example of "encouragement": Ever go to an HR conference? That's where the darkness grows in exponential levels. You wouldn't think this would be the case. However, people rarely talk about the people in their organizations that are great. They talk openly and colorfully about those people who seem to consume the majority of their thoughts and actions. In fact, if you stop conversations and ask HR folks to share stories about people who rock, it throws them because it just isn't the norm.

The key to owning this reality of our companies and their cultures is not to feel that swimming upstream is wrong. We are called to swim upstream and go against the flow. A great quote that I use in my presentations and put on my office wall is "Only dead fish go with the flow."

Only
dead
fish go
with
the
flow.

Nonconformity makes us uncomfortable as HR professionals. We have been "raised" to put things in order and do our best to eliminate variability. It's time for us to understand that conformity kills diversity. The more we strive to make things uniform and homogenous, the more we eliminate innovation, performance, and creativity from our environment.

You see, the dark side of HR may only be that people are different. Do you spend time with people who are different from you intentionally, or do you surround yourself with those who look like you, think like you, and act like you? We make the workplace dim and dull when we keep such a narrow comfort zone. I know several HR peers who avoid spending more of their day with "difficult" people because it is so disconcerting to them. We don't take the time to get to know why, or if, a person is difficult. We just don't like that some people fall outside the norms.

In my opinion, "diversity" had to become a program and a set of initiatives in our organizations because we refused to swim among our people. We've also defined diversity more along the lines of compliance with the list of categories of people from the Equal Employment Opportunity Commission (EEOC). Quick side note: If you're allowing behavior and treatment of others that runs counter to EEOC guidance, then that's not a lack of being diverse—it's breaking the law.

People are naturally diverse, and that makes them amazing!! We all come from different cultures, heritages, family structures, education, economic levels, and life experiences. We're like a giant knot of characteristics that is intertwined and not easily able to be categorized. It would be great to see that our differences make us stronger. This belief needs to be foundational to HR and in our workplaces. Instead of becoming frustrated with differences, we should explore them and allow them to flourish.

To do this, you have to go against the flow.

I mentioned earlier that I grew up in Ada, Ohio. My graduating class consisted of 73 people. The school I attended was so small that I knew all the students and teachers in every grade. Even in a tiny, rural school people fall into separate peer groups. These groups existed before I went to school, and they still do. You know them—the jocks, the band/choir geeks, the nerds, the popular kids, and the fringe kids. The labels may have changed over time, but the groups still form. There is incredible pressure for you to join in one group so that you "belong."

I never understood this. You see, I was connected to every group possible at school. I played basketball, was the band equipment manager, took every science and math course I could, sang in the show choir, and served as president of my class for two years as well as in the student council. I did this because I wanted to be with every student and not just ones in a certain group. I never pitted one group against another, but I did take heat from strong members of each group to make a choice and leave the other groups. I refused.

Now, you could make the argument that I was in a small school that allowed me to join various groups, and large schools wouldn't have given me that freedom. Not true. I did this in college, and

I've continued to do this in every organization where I've worked. I enjoy floating between departments, facilities, and locations. It is freeing to meet and talk with the front-line staff as much as it is to sit in a board room with executives.

The pressure to conform and join groups is as prevalent in companies as it was in high school. You have to realize this and swim across the boundaries. Be different yourself in your actions, and spend time with the others who are different from you. Learn about each other, and then pull all of these great differences together to make that intertwined knot of people grow, thrive, and perform!!

CHAPTER 13

DON'T LET THE CEMENT DRY

I FONDLY REMEMBER building a half-court basketball court at my house in my hometown. My dad was geeked about me playing basketball. He had played himself when he was younger. He asked me if I was serious about playing. I said I was, and he said that we should build a place where I could practice. Please note that this was long before the practice today where you have traveling teams and tryouts, and the Amateur Athletic Union (AAU) system of select amateur players was something that may have existed in big cities, but not out in the country.

My dad has always been a great role model of how "real work" is to be done. He gave my brother and me each a spade and pointed at the grass that had to be removed for the court to come to life. We had no idea what to do with a spade, and this was just the beginning of this construction effort. As with most dads, he let out a heavy sigh, shook his head and snatched the spade out of my hand.

"Look, you do it like this," he proclaimed as the steel blade cut a horizontal patch of sod.

He lifted it effortlessly and ripped a huge chunk of the lawn into the air and gently laid it to the side. He asked if we understood and grunted that we needed to get started. The sod stripping took hours, and then we had to level the ground before the worst task came to be.

Have you ever mixed cement? I'm not talking Quikrete that just needs to have water added to it, and it magically sets up with little effort. I'm talking about making it from "scratch." I have done this. We took the cement mix, a large trough, and five-gallon buckets of water. The mixing alone almost made my arms come out of their sockets. Did I mention that I was 13 years old and lacked any muscle formation at this point in my life?

I can hear my dad's voice as I continued to stir. "Don't let the cement dry!! It's no good if it dries in the trough."

I'll be honest—I didn't care if that cement dried in the trough. I was about to drop. When he saw that I had hit my physical limit, he stepped in and worked magic. The dust, rocks, and water came together and made a slurry that was able to be poured into the freshly stripped ground. We worked for 12 hours to get the ground ready and the court laid out.

As I fell into bed, my Dad came into my room and said, "Good work today. It feels good to get your hands dirty, doesn't it? We'll start again tomorrow."

It did feel good.

We took another week to finish the court because we put a fence up to block any errant basketballs from flying into the neighbor's yard. We also painted the posts, fence, and court to the exact dimensions you'd find in a gym. The finishing touch was when my dad put spotlights on the roof of the house so we could practice at any time of day or night.

At the end of the project, I thanked my dad for the phenomenal court. I couldn't believe that he had invested so much in my inter-est that I had just started to pursue. He has always been someone to share his wisdom with me. When we were done, he shared this: "Remember, hard work means getting your hands dirty. Always respect the work that people do."

Now, I have to admit that as an HR professional, I have it pretty good. I go to an office, sit behind a desk, and have the technology and resources to do my job. This has been true in every role that I've had in HR. I'm thankful for that, but I don't take it for granted.

It's very easy for us to lose sight of employees that get their hands dirty because we have allowed the separation of levels in organi-zations. We tend to strain our necks looking up either to get senior management's attention or to jump at its beck and call for the hope of more face time. We can easily forget that the vast majority of employees are performing regular tasks. Too often these folks are overlooked or are seen as people who are expendable. It's not "hard" to replace them—or so we mistakenly think.

It's intriguing to me that if people rise through an organization because of their performance or promotion, they quickly forget the position or level they once held. They look down on others who are below them. It's an unfortunate reality in the cultures of our organizations. HR plays along and never sheds light on this inequity. This is greater than job description, title, or compensation. This is devaluing people and the contributions they make.

When this delineation of people occurs, you'll hear it in how they describe themselves. When you ask what role they have, they say, "I'm just a _____" (fill in the role).

This is unacceptable. There should be no "just a" roles in your company.

The only way this disappears is if HR steps in and takes notice of all employees and what they do. It is our chance to validate who they are and the efforts they give daily. It's not their fault that they are ignored. This is unfortunately ingrained into how we work.

People want to come in and give their best. They don't sit at home waiting to come into the office, store, or plant just waiting to be destructive and tear down things. **SOMEONE** has to start believing in people again. They are longing for it, and they desperately want to have a person who will represent and champion them. It's missing, and if you step in to be the person, or department, who bridges this gap, you'll truly differentiate your company from the majority of the work landscape.

Remember: Always respect the work that people do.

The cement is still wet in your organization. You need to step in and make sure it doesn't get dry.

CHAPTER 14

SHOW. DO. REVIEW.

EVERY SINGLE COMPANY struggles with two major components: communication and training. It doesn't matter if you're from a *Fortune* 100 global entity or a local, small business. Few organizations do these two things consistently or well. As work environments become more and more technology driven, communication and training are going to be even more challenging. This isn't a rant against technology. Far from it.

HR needs to come to terms that technology is the norm. It always has been, but the pace of it is so fast and staggering that we are now hesitant, reluctant, or avoidant. You need to know that if you choose to step away from HR technology, social media, artificial intelligence, and the like—others won't. Since these are now realities of how communication and work occur, we need to position ourselves to be in the midst of all that's going on.

One thing won't change when it comes to communication and training: the human factor. People are still the ones who generate messages and receive them. The methods and forums they use fluctuate on a constant basis, but communication still occurs. In fact, it's occurring at an extremely rapid pace with much higher volumes of information and data being shared and consumed. How can we keep up without being overwhelmed or swallowed by this incessant wave?

It begins by simplifying what we do and how we communicate.

HR is notorious when it comes to burying others with pages and pages of manuals, training guides, and processes. An old boss told me once that I reminded him of a college professor who felt the pressure to "publish or perish." Sound familiar? Many HR practitioners feel that if they aren't cranking out material then they aren't being effective or valued. It's an unfortunate trap that we have built over the years. This approach has been passed on for generations within our workforce. Instead of removing layers, we add a new revision date and then republish to make sure things are current and in people's hands.

The volume of communication that HR and organizations in general produce has a limited effect compared with the results that are desired. Do the following sentences sound familiar?

"We sent out the e-mail a week ago."

"The posters were issued with instructions for everyone to remove the old ones and put up the new ones."

"We had a class on that topic, and everyone signed in, and they passed the quiz at the end of the session."

I'd wager you could fill an entire book with phrases showing how the intended communication fell short of its goal. Instead of reevaluating how things happened, we churn and churn in an endless circle of frustration to try to "fix" what we did. The same cyclical model can be said of training.

We may use new platforms and electronic versions of classes to give employees the chance to take the course when and where they want, but the training still doesn't stick. We're confused by this because the vendor promised that we'd see improved productivity and engagement. The first step is to reconfigure, rewrite, and have MANDATORY training sessions reverting back to a 20' x 20' classroom with rows of seats and a 450-slide deck on an outdated version of PowerPoint.

I'm not trying to be sarcastic. It's the model I was taught and what I've used. I think we all want to see communication and training improve. If it did, then employees would actually be equipped to perform, and our messages would be sent and received with clarity. It sounds utopian because we refuse to take the one initial step to address the shortcomings of these two critical organizational areas.

When you ask people for the **ONE** thing they would like in their jobs more than anything, the answer is—more time. It never fails. The rapid pace of communication and technology washes over us, and we feel as if we're barely keeping our head above water. This is another trap that we've come to believe as truth. People honestly have plenty of time to perform their job, communicate well, and develop others. What gets in the way is "how" we use our time. People have time each day to be focused, keep healthy, and enjoy things outside of work. However, our inability to be intentional and our constant running after every alarm bell keeps us from doing this.

Here's a new method that HR needs to do itself, own, and teach others when it comes to communication and training:

First—breathe.

Second—calm down and clear your head.

Third—try a new model. Show. Do. Review.

We have to come to terms with the fact that few things are so critical that we can't step back and evaluate how things are/aren't going. Seriously. Unless you're in a profession where timing is essential for success, you have time. If you would do this more often and build time into your schedule, you'd realize that much of what you do is redundant and could be streamlined and simplified. Skeptical? Try this out as an exercise ...

Look at the last five e-mails you sent, and pretend you're the receiver instead of the sender.

Would you know what to do based on each e-mail? Is the message clear and concise? Does it ramble on for lines and lines to make sure that every angle was captured and considered?

The truth is you don't know. We all are phenomenal senders, but we rarely take the time to review the intent of our communication, the audience receiving it, and whether it really matters to what needs to be accomplished. Stepping back and taking a breath to clear our head and stop the noise is a simple enough thing to try, but it takes incredible discipline. It doesn't just happen. It needs your attention and effort.

The same rings true with training. Instead of using a "Show. Do. Review." approach, we tend to follow a "Tell. Tell again. Get frustrated. Tell again." approach.

There's a great example of how this simple method, done well, can improve communication and set the stage for how training should occur.

I work for a family pizzeria. When we hire new team members for our special events crews, they have usually never worked with food. I meet with all of the new hires and conduct their orientation, fill out their paperwork, and introduce them to the culture of our company. I make sure that the orientation is high energy, exciting, and interactive. The manager of special events follows me and gets them even more geeked about what they're going to be doing at the various venues and community festivals around the city. He's even more high energy than I am (which is hard to do if you know me).

Just after the newbies feel charged about something they've never done, they leave our orientation room and move to a pizza table with two other team members who will be their supervisors. They are much more patient and even-keeled than the manager and I are. They calmly instruct each new employee how to take a dough, spread sauce over it evenly, and add pepperoni and cheese before putting it on the oven conveyor. As the pizza travels through the 500-degree heat, the supervisors ask the newbies how it felt to make their first pizza. There are a mix of shrugs, comments that it was pretty easy, and a sense of relief that they didn't make a mistake.

When the piping-hot pizza emerges from the oven, the supervisors teach the team members to pull out the pizza, put it in a box, and cut it into slices. After the newbies finish this process, the supervisors close the lid on the box and say, "Here you go. You've made your first pizza of many. Welcome to the team!!"

You should see these people rush to their cars to go home and tell their family about their experience and show them their work. It's amazing to witness. The special events crew has some of the highest retention in the company, and they use the method of show, do, review every day with every team member.

When we realized we could step back, evaluate how things were going, and then decide on a path that would work, we changed from a very traditional and cumbersome method of onboarding to what we do now. This model works at all levels of an organization and with every type of task. The challenge that faces HR is this: Are we willing to be different and simplify training and communication?

It works. Try it and see!!

CHAPTER 15

KEEP IT SIMPLE

I'VE SEEN HUMAN RESOURCES EVOLVE over my career. It's the only industry and profession that I've been in for 30-plus years. It's fascinating to see what started as personnel is now focused on talent and humanizing the workplace.

One thing that has unfortunately become a stereotype of HR is the stacks and stacks of layers that we add to everything we touch. There has been, and continues to be, a tendency to create massive programs, manuals, policies, and procedures to make sure that every possible work situation is captured, identified, and categorized. It's tiring and cumbersome. No wonder more people leave HR than stay in the profession.

This doesn't have to be our approach or how we should be defined. However, it takes a very intentional personal step to break with tradition and go against the flow. Most HR people are more content to ride the stream and deftly negotiate the ebbs and flows of people and organizations. What I'm going to suggest is that you jump out of your boat of comfort and fully immerse yourself in changing how HR is practiced.

Employee engagement is where I want you to start. It is a reality of organizations that the more employees are engaged in what they do in their roles, the more likely they are to perform, stay with the company, and even encourage others to join them. A multitude of blogs, webinars, conferences, and presentations promise to improve engagement in your company. People either offer a "silver bullet" approach or a five- to seven-step guarantee that never fails.

Neither works. We're talking about people, not another programmatic effort.

It astonishes me that companies are willing to invest thousands of dollars in some off-the-shelf program to get people to be more engaged. If one attempt fails, we are tasked with finding the next, great vendor that will make it stick—this time. The endless cycle of churning is another stereotype and pitfall of HR in organizations, and it has to stop.

The radical step I'm encouraging you to consider, and then act on, is to simplify your approach.

Reading this, you're probably thinking that simplification is an easy out or a way to cut corners. It's some sort of HR shtick or parlor trick that won't yield legitimate, measurable results. I beg to differ and can show you an example of how simplification works and continues to evolve.

The way I define "engagement" is this: The more employees are connected to the work they do and to the organization as a whole, the more engaged they are.

That's it. Now, producing this connectivity takes extensive, intentional effort and a willingness to redefine the norms within a company culture. It goes against every fiber of how you've been taught as an HR professional and how others practice in more traditional ways. You see, we tend to jump to the desired result we want (employee engagement), and we rush through the steps we could take to involve employees and connect them to the company.

Let me show you how it can work: I work for a regional family pizzeria that has been in business for 60-plus years in the Greater Cincinnati area. The company is a local icon and a staple of the community. We have great team members, and we wanted to make sure we recognized them for all that they do for us.

We had practiced traditional recognition of our team members based on their years of service by having a massive, formal sit-down dinner at a local conference center. Remember that we have people who work in shifts on various days and at various times. No two team members work the same schedule. However, we asked them all to meet us at a location that wasn't their place of work at a time convenient to corporate leadership (me included).

Don't get me wrong: The banquets were wonderful when it came to the feel, environment, food, and the personal recognition given to folks who had reached 5, 10, 15, 20, 25, 30, 35, and 40 years of service. However, after every banquet, the corporate leaders and the team members felt that it was somewhat "icky" (that's an official HR term). We were going through the motions of recognition, but it didn't reflect the warm, inviting, family-oriented culture of our restaurants and our brand.

One year the day after yet another recognition soiree, my boss came to my office and said, "This doesn't feel right. Everything seems forced, and people are uncomfortable. I want you to change it so that we're truly recognizing our people."

I asked if I had any boundaries or if I could be creative in doing this. He said that I had a clean slate, but that it had to be sustainable and matter to people. Not an easy task. My staff and I looked at various options and ideas, but each became just as layered and cumbersome as what we were doing. So I took the step to simplify it and strip it down completely.

The program that I came up with is to give team members a gift card that they could use however they choose, a card from the CEO and president thanking them for their years of service, balloons, and a bag of smiley-face cookies. You see, our culture follows the mantra to "Reach Out and Make Smiles," so the cookies worked.

The second, and most critical, component of this program is that I visit team members during their shift regardless of the time, location, or date they work. I want to thank them for the work they do at their workplace because that is where they have performed their work for at least the past five years.

My boss loves it, and it has been our recognition program ever since. In fact, team members at our locations now anticipate receiving their cookies and wonder when that guy from HR is coming to visit. We have grand celebrations that are personal, one-on-one, and genuine. I've experienced reactions ranging from surprise to warm hugs, and even tears. All for balloons and cookies.

Employees will **NEVER** be engaged unless HR is engaged first and models that engagement by taking it directly to where the employees work. The model takes a ton of my time, but it's worth every moment.

Step back, HR, from what you're currently doing when it comes to recognition. Deconstruct it and evaluate what you're really doing when you recognize employees. People are yearning to be acknowledged for who they are and what they do. Engage them by being engaged yourself. When you do, you will transform them and your organization.

CHAPTER 16

WHAT ABOUT YOU?

WHEN I WAS 13 YEARS OLD, I moved to a new town. At the time, I didn't think things could get much worse: a new town with a new school and absolutely no friends. Piled on top of this avalanche of change, adolescence was in full bloom, and I had a new step-dad. My parents have always been supportive and encouraging, and I'm thankful for that. They suggested that I try out for the seventh-grade football team because all the boys at the school tried out.

I showed up at the first day of tryouts and was already unprepared before the first activity that took place. I didn't have the best shoes to run in, and my gym clothes looked completely out-of-date compared with clothes on the wave of other boys who showed up. You have to know that this town (which I now adore) is the type of town where every family knows each other for generations and all the boys at tryouts had been going to school together since kindergarten. I couldn't have been more of an outlier if I had tried.

I wanted to run away back across town to my home, but I stuck it out. I tried to introduce myself to other boys, but I only got screamed at by the overzealous coach who could string together profanity like an art form. The first day of football tryouts consisted of a series of sadistic drills and exercises to determine our "fitness." I kept up with my peers but didn't feel comfortable with how the coach was treating everyone. This feeling culminated when we were supposed to do 100 sit-ups in the blazing sun after we had been doing drills for over one and one-half hours with no water break. I was exhausted and wondered why in the world I was subjecting myself to this torture. As I tried to keep doing sit-ups, the coach leaned over me and screamed a line of obscenities that made his face turn red while every vein bulged out of his forehead. He hit me in the stomach as I was laying back between sit-ups. I ran toward the school building and bent over to wretch.

Great first day in front of my peers. I left the practice and never played a down of football. Ever. Just my luck, the football coach turned out to be my art teacher that fall. I despised him and never forgot how he treated me or others.

My first day of actual classes in junior high was miserably awkward as well. The assistant principal came out in the hallway as I wandered aimlessly trying to find my classroom. He asked me if everything was okay, and I choked up and cried. He was empathetic and asked if I was playing football. I didn't have the heart to share my miserable experience, so I just shook my head "No."

He said, "That's great."

I was perplexed. Why was it great that I wasn't with what seemed like every boy in my grade? I wanted to desperately belong, not stand out.

He continued, "You're awful tall for your age. How tall are you?"

I answered, "I'm 6 feet tall" (remember I was 13 and now attending a small-town school where all grades, K-12, were in one building).

He was so supportive!! "Excellent. Do you like basketball? I'd like you to come to conditioning tomorrow with the varsity basketball team. Let's get you connected."

The next day I was in the gym with all the boys who focused on basketball and not football. I played, and excelled, in basketball from seventh grade through my senior year. The assistant principal was my coach for three of those years, and the teams I was on won our conference five of the six years I played. One year we came one basket from going to the state championship. I was so fortunate the assistant principal caught me wandering in the hallway.

What does this have to do with HR? Everything.

The two coaches exemplify how companies look at professional development. Organizations take one of two paths. They either make development forced and uncomfortable, or they have a broader view of allowing people to develop their strengths. The sad thing is that, as HR professionals, we tend to fall into the forced category both personally and in how we structure development for others throughout the company.

We often tie development to performance reviews and want people to hone their skills in various areas. However, the classes and training sessions we want them to attend are more likely to address their gaps or "weaknesses." It's just like punching them in the stomach during sit-ups. They're already not good in certain areas, so let's take the tact of forcing training to make them more well-rounded.

It's okay to see if people can learn skills in areas in which they may not be as strong, but it shouldn't be the focus of development. Working from people's strengths is more natural and helps them grow and add even more value in their roles. This is a break with how organizations view development, but I contend that working from a person's strengths is more effective, sustainable, and relevant.

An additional component is woefully absent in professional development: HR professionals don't seek development themselves. We spend so much time and effort making sure others are taken care of, but we don't develop ourselves. Feedback and research cite that many people in executive leadership roles are concerned because HR professionals don't have a comprehensive knowledge of their own field. This is unacceptable.

We can't keep yearning to be included and seen as businesspeople if we are lacking in what we know about HR. I understand that our field is dynamic, fast paced, and ever evolving. Since that is the norm, we have to be well equipped and prepared to excel in HR as one of our strengths. After we have HR under our belt and are able to be the go-to resource in our company, then we absolutely should add all facets of business, including marketing, finance, operations, and sales. There's no area that you can't tackle.

Let me be the coach who meets you in the hallway.

It's time to stop wandering professionally and join the team. That team is the greater HR community. You should become a voracious reader of HR and business blogs and books. Go to conferences where you can not only hone your HR skills but attend sessions that stretch you to see where the field is going. Add skills that you can use to improve yourself and your company. Join HR organizations nationally and locally. Get connected to other HR professionals on purpose. Seek your professional certification in HR.

Personal aside if you'll be so kind:

I highly recommend that you join, and become active in, the Society for Human Resource Management (SHRM) nationally and locally. It provides the most comprehensive certification in HR, which is competency-based and is closely associated to how HR is truly practiced. Please note that I put this in because I am a connected and active member of SHRM who has my SHRM certification. As stated earlier in the book, I want to model the behavior I'd like to see in others.

There's no need to be passive in any of these efforts.

We all need to keep in mind that if we don't consciously develop ourselves on an ongoing basis throughout our careers, we will slowly become irrelevant. When we become irrelevant, the company doesn't need us or what we do. Staying relevant is the biggest threat we face as an industry.

Build the time in your schedule and your career for professional development. It makes you a stronger professional, leader, and resource.

CHAPTER 17

CHECKERS OR CHESS?

IN ALL THE ROLES we assume throughout our career, we have a boss. We often make comments about whom we report to, and those are usually negative. Even the best boss-subordinate relationships tend to focus on the frustrating points. The unfortunate positioning organizationally of one role being "above" the other one almost automatically pits one against the other.

This organizational component is true regardless of department or level within a company. An innate tension extends from the front line all the way to the CEO. Rarely do we take time to reflect on these relationships, which is odd because they make up the infrastructure of almost every organizational model. It's time for us to step back, look at the boss-subordinate relationship, and determine if it's healthy or destructive. The reason to do this is that the sum of the various reporting relationships and organizational chart reporting duties comprise the framework of the culture of your company. How those relationships either work well together or work against each other has a ripple effect that permeates people's interactions.

I have been fortunate. Throughout my career I've predominantly had great bosses. Even the ones who weren't the best fits for me gave me plenty of experiences that I learned from. Maybe I didn't particularly care for a behavior or approach, but I kept my interactions with those bosses in mind to refine how I have worked with others. Also, for the majority of my career I was an HR department of one. So I have always had a boss, but I didn't have direct reports myself until my current position. This is true of many folks in our profession. Therefore, the relationship I have had with my direct supervisor has always been key in how I practiced HR.

The great bosses I have had ranged from a person who retired six months after I started, to an entrepreneur who was wildly creative, to a self-made woman who rose to an executive role through her mixture of intelligence and intentionality, to a person who started working at an organization in high school and remained there for 40-plus years.

My most recent boss-subordinate relationship has been a healthy one. When I first started with the company, he made time in his schedule for a weekly one-on-one meeting with me. Our second meeting he dropped this nugget of wisdom on me.

"Steve, next week when we get together, I'm going to share my expectations of you and HR for our company. And I would like you to come back with your expectations of me as your boss."

I sat across from him stupefied. This is not the best way to make a positive impression when you're just starting with a company. I had never heard this at any other point of my career. I was used to my supervisor telling me what he or she expected and how to maneuver through projects and an endless array of ever-changing project deadlines. It was so odd that he wanted my thoughts about OUR working relationship. I actually struggled coming up with a list for our next meeting because it was such a different approach. When we reconvened, he flustered me again.

"Did you bring your list?" I nodded that I did. "Great, you go first."

Again, I sat there dumbfounded. What did he mean that I got to share first? Was this some sort of trap or landmine? What if my expectations were silly to him? Even worse, what if I pushed too far? The questions swirled and swirled in my head filling me with massive amounts of anxiety. I took a deep breath and shared what I hoped for our relationship. He took notes and didn't really respond until I finished. Then, he replied, "I can do that. Great meeting."

I didn't understand what kind of mind tricks he was playing. Where was his list? Did it complement mine or run counter to what I offered? I felt lost and somewhat apprehensive about how things would move forward. I had never reported to someone who was this open, sought my opinion, and then took my suggestions to heart. It was refreshing, but I was skeptical. I just wasn't sure that I could perform in this nontraditional top-down relationship.

The following week he told me that he had wanted to think over what I had shared and not just have a knee-jerk reaction before sharing his expectations. He and I were going to have a relationship that complemented each of our outlooks on people and the organization and on how to integrate HR across the entire enterprise. His leadership was unlike most I've encountered, and it has changed the way I work.

What is your boss-subordinate relationship like? Is it healthy like this one has been? If it isn't, are you tolerating it, or are you just putting your head down as you reluctantly trudge through each day? One other thing: What about you? Are you a boss of others? What is the relationship you have with your direct reports?

Not focusing on the relationships between supervisors and their direct reports has been a huge miss in organizations. HR tries to mend or nurture relationships between people on a daily basis. It's as if we have a quasi-counselor role. However, we spend so much time in triage mode trying to maintain a stable work environment for people that we never get a chance to step back to gauge the effectiveness and health of relationships. The reason for this is that we practice HR as if we're playing checkers.

What?? Yes, checkers.

During one of my weekly meetings, my boss asked me about this. He always has some nugget for me to chew on, and I appreciate that he does his best to develop me. Recently he asked me if I practiced HR playing checkers or chess. I wasn't sure where he was going with this, so I took the bait. I chose not to answer directly and returned with the question, "Which one should I be doing?"

He explained which game made more sense for my role personally and for the organization. Can you guess which one? It's chess.

HR practitioners who practice as if they're playing checkers move in straight lines either forward or backward. They are more concerned with "getting things done" so they can reach the other side of the board and get rewarded. This is much more of a short-term, task-oriented approach. It may have bursts of success, and we're able to cross tasks off lists, but the pace never ends. It's a narrow way to practice what we do and can be very frustrating. If things occur that aren't in a task format, we may halt and not move at all.

HR played like chess is much different. This approach takes into account multiple players who have various skills. It also acknowledges that the return move by the other team will not be predictable. HR as chess involves strategy and various ways to conduct counter moves throughout the game. You can position yourself well and look ahead at what may happen. True, you may suffer losses and setbacks, but it doesn't mean that you'll be defeated. Moreover, all members of your team can accomplish tasks—using their strengths.

The other primary reason to approach HR as a chess game is that you're going to be playing with other departments that may have to play checkers. How can you bring a long-term, strategic approach to those who are task oriented? I think the key is being agile and adaptable. I'm not talking about designing or developing a massive publication. This is more hands-on and requires you to make the moves on the board, which is where they're happening anyway.

I've always enjoyed working in environments where items are produced. It's interesting when you go out on the floor with people who play checkers. They look at you and don't think you "work" because they can see the results of their efforts as a piece comes off the line or the pizza comes out of the oven. They see you walking around thinking that you're just wasting time. What they miss is that the time walking around is spent in observation, relationship-building, and acknowledgement of the value of their efforts. Over time, these subtle actions weave chess moves that build culture, affect how people treat each other, and give employees someone to connect with as an anchor to the organization.

Which game do you play currently? Trust me when I say that you need to evaluate and determine which one it is. It's difficult to try to keep either of them as a hybrid because you will tend to drift toward what is more comfortable versus what is more challenging.

Chess takes time, thought, and risks. We continue to think that if we pursue these characteristics in our job, we aren't "really working." That just isn't true. HR practitioners taking time to be thoughtful in their approach is essential to being relevant. Looking out over the board and seeing what your move will do while anticipating what the counter maneuver could be is how work occurs every day. In chess you have to take risks to move forward.

All employees are either checkers players or chess players. This is especially true for bosses. Most are checkers players, and it's how they've been recognized and advanced in the company. We in HR can't afford to be checkers players. We have to see across the entire organization to know who's moving where and then be able to make the necessary adjustment to encounter those employees and help them stay engaged.

Making the switch to chess is needed and fulfilling. Let me leave you with this:

Pawn to E4. Now it's your move.

CHAPTER 18

PASSION IS NOT A DIRTY WORD

HAVE YOU EVER GONE through the motions at work? You know the routine. You take your commute using the same route at the same time hoping for no unexpected delays. The scenery zips by you in a blur of muted colors that have no real form or shape. Some run-of-the-mill song from some familiar artist that you've heard a million times is droning from either the radio or your headphones. It's comforting noise because it blocks out the drivers around you. When you actually arrive at your destination you don't even truly recall what happened to get you from your residence to your office.

Sounds inspirational, doesn't it? The challenge is that this is the feeling of most people going to work every day. There is little variation in the routine. Few fight it, and most look at how the flow is moving and for a place to join in. The modern working landscape involves employees traveling back and forth to make sure they put in their time doing tasks over and over and over as if on an infinite treadmill.

The vast majority of our adult life is spent working. When we think of the description above, we sink into our seats at our desks just a bit more each day. One distraction to this malaise is to complain about the mediocrity we face with others. We in HR are the employees who grouse just as much as the others we point our fingers toward. Ugh.

How does this routine take shape? This isn't some rhetorical philosophy. It's the burdensome reality of workplaces around the globe. We have the opportunity every day to break out of the mundane, but we put little effort toward making that happen. I remember growing up as a kid seeing a picture of the prehistoric wooly mammoth fighting to get out of the La Brea Tar Pits in California. The predators that forced the mammoth into the tar are waiting for it to be defenseless so they can pounce and get their pound of flesh. Again—sound like work?

The cultures of many organizations are either adversarial or filled with so much peer pressure that people succumb to the forces around them. The joy, energy, and enthusiasm people innately have are slowly beaten out of them so that they can be "productive" and do "good work." It's disheartening. It's also not what work should be—ever!!

Have you ever been around little kids? They are fantastic. They really are. Everything around them is a new experience. They don't miss a thing, and they have few preconceptions about what things do, how they work, or what will happen when they interact with them. Kids also have this same approach with people. They are fascinated by others. Kids will ask you questions that are completely inappropriate just to get to know you better. Their inquisitiveness often frustrates adults, but they carry on undaunted. They have to know everything about you because they're trying to understand what makes you unique.

Earlier in the book I noted that when kids grow up, they become our employees. The tragic facet of this transformation is that we beat the child out of our employees to make them workers. The attributes that made them explore the world around them are pushed out so that they fit neatly into roles, job descriptions, and salary grades. The other tragic aspect of this transformation is that we're okay with this as HR professionals. It doesn't faze us in the least. In fact, we expect people to become automatons that master certain functions in order to keep stability and normality in the workplace. When someone steps out of this environment, we act to return him or her back to the corral.

When I was a freshman in college, I sang in a group that toured and performed during our spring break in towns throughout Ohio. I enjoyed being a part of this group of college students because we had much in common—or so I assumed. Usually after we performed a concert, the families who hosted us provided us a potluck meal. This was fantastic because, as a college student, any free food was good food. After our first event, the choir gathered with the families we performed for, and we went through the buffet line filling our plates.

The little kids who attended with their parents sat at a separate table that was lower to the ground and had chairs that fit their young stature. As my fellow singers finished selecting their food, they all rushed to sit with the adults. No one was sitting with the kids. Evidently they wanted to be associated with, and seen as, adults. They wanted to fit in with the norms of what they thought was expected of them. I get it, and I understand the pressure to feel accepted. So I turned to the kids table and sat down at the head of their table.

Now, you have to understand something that made this look even more out of place than it already was. I'm 6'4" and not a small person. When I sat down with the kids, my knees were up to my chest, and I dwarfed all of them. We had a blast together!! They giggled and laughed that I looked so disproportionate. It was a laugh riot. We talked about everything that popped into their beautiful minds. Very little content of our conversation made sense. We shared food and dessert, and by the time I was done eating, they were crawling all over me like a human jungle gym. It was spectacular.

My peers couldn't believe that I sat with the kids instead of the adults. In fact, after dinner before we left for the night, a "meeting" was called. The meeting was about me and my behavior. I was a bit perplexed and oblivious to anything being unconventional or inappropriate about what I did. Evidently I was not representing the school or the choir well and was informed that this type of abhorrent action would no longer be tolerated.

One other thing you need to know about me—I don't sit well with people making overarching generalizations and stereotypes. I never have. I pushed back instantly and asked why what I did was "wrong." The answers were perfect. You see, my peers had already prepared themselves for being in the workforce and they didn't even realize it yet.

I was told that it wasn't right that I was laughing during a meal. Also, another atrocity that came to light was that I was playing and paying attention to kids instead of the adults who were kind enough to prepare a meal for me. As the litany of behaviors were cited, I started to laugh out loud. This only made the leaders of the choir who called this meeting even more impatient and frustrated.

I said, "You're mad because I was enjoying myself, having fun with others, and laughing. That's the problem that needs to be addressed?"

The leaders nodded. I replied, "That's sad. You see, the kids had more life than anyone sitting in that room, including all of you. I choose to be around people who enjoy life and have passion. I thought that's who we were supposed to be."

I was told to grow up and change my ways. After the next concert, I sat at the kids table again—and three others joined me. By the end of the tour, the choir asked me if I would be their leader my sophomore year. I turned them down and walked away. I probably shouldn't have done that, but I wanted to make the point once again that expressing passion is not something that should be discouraged.

I've held to that principle, and it's been one of the foundational blocks of practicing HR. It kills me that I see others in human resources who don't want to jump to the kid's table because they see it as a waste of time and effort. We've lost our love for what we do and who we impact. It is slowly tearing down the profession, and it's resulting in more negativity to be our calling card and expectation.

It's time for us to change our approach. If you're not passionate about HR, get out. Change careers. Seriously. Not a joke.

We see "passion" as something that leads to a possible harassment claim. We've lost the glow and luster of how awesome human resources is as a job and as an industry. The excitement and burning desire you had when you first started HR has dwindled to a small, flickering ember. Is that how you want to practice or be seen? I know it's not true for me.

Passion within HR drives me to be in the midst of people more and more every day. It never gets dimmed or quenched. People try to snuff out the passion just like my peers did in college. Whenever that pushback comes, I become even **MORE** passionate.

You need this as your foundation block. It's not an option. Passion is not a dirty word—it's essential.

CHAPTER 19

BE FULL

PEOPLE ARE EXHAUSTING, aren't they? Everyone in HR thinks and feels this, but we don't dare say it out loud. We're expected to wear a mask that says we have an unlimited ability to meet, empathize with, and handle any person for any reason. It's a lie, and we need to be more honest about this unspoken reality and have a healthier method to combat it.

One great thing about being completely wiped out and exhausted is that it clears your head. You don't have the energy to take on even one more situation no matter how small it is. When I've hit this stage at work (and it's happened more than once over my career), I've stepped back and reflected on what factors led me to the point of exhaustion.

Here's a great idea to ponder: Do you notice what most people say when you ask them how things are? The vast majority of them say, "I'm busy." There's never really a definition of what that means other than they apparently have a ton of things on their mind or taking up the majority of their focus. This is true with every employee we meet every day. It never fails. People are either "good" or "busy." We take that as an acceptable answer and just move on. We don't take the time to stop and ask them to explain their response.

Now, I know it's just a word, but when I hear people say they are "busy," I hear a negative tone behind it. It seems that when you're busy, you have things that "have" to get done even though you may not enjoy doing them. Being busy also implies that you are overwhelmed and feel that others don't share your sentiment. It's the feeling that no one could be as busy as you are. It's just not possible that any other person on the planet can adequately understand everything that is going on in your life personally or professionally. Having this approach is a bit daunting. The reason is that **EVERYONE** is busy!!

A few years ago, I changed my answer when people asked me how I was. If you ask me, my answer is "I'm full." It's true. I am. I take the chance to fill my life up every single day with things that are positive, challenging, and interesting.

Don't get me wrong, there are things that fill up my life that I'd like to change. I get upset too often and frustrated more than I should. I watch too much TV and don't eat as well as I should. Those are facts that I can work on. They could be things that pull you down, but they don't have to be.

To be honest, I think I could even add a few more things in to make my life even fuller. You aren't any different. Your life is full too. The question you have to ask yourself is this: Do you like what your life is filled with?

Most HR folks I know always share how busy they are. When I hear this, I can sense the frustration and angst they feel about their work. What people don't see is that if they keep the "busy" mentality, they'll never enjoy HR because they'll always be chasing after the things they don't enjoy doing.

It's time for you to become full instead. Take the time to review what you're doing, and strip away those things that pull you down. I understand that all work has its purpose. How you approach that work is the key. Having the satisfaction that your efforts are filling your days will make you see things from a much brighter viewpoint. Once you've mastered this positive response, it's time to teach others.

We've missed a reality about ourselves and our employees: the issue of capacity. We have the misconception that all employees want to become the next CEO. We rarely fill them up with the work they currently do. People have space that needs to be filled. We don't take the time to have people evaluate if the work they do adds value. They may be getting things done, but do those efforts matter? The majority of the work completed in organizations, and especially in HR, is done out of comfort and repetition. It's natural for people to veer from work that could help them grow and be fulfilled in order to stay in a comfortable pattern.

Helping employees identify and work at their fullest capacity is an area of opportunity for HR to excel. We are stuck in the rut of measuring performance and accepting mediocrity. This is reflected in the growing discontent of people in their jobs. The traditional approach is to develop the next great trend, practice, theme, or flavor of the month to get people energized. It hasn't worked and never will.

Capacity filling is the answer. The more fully functioning you are in your role in HR, the more you can model how this can be the reality of employees regardless of their level within the organization. Executives and front-line folks alike aren't at their capacity. Another assumption that limits us strategically is that we assume that senior management has everything figured out and that everything is going well. Our focus and effort are almost always on the middle and lower levels of companies. There has been great work in organizational development that encourages a borderless, collaborative workforce, but we still live in the world of hierarchy. Because that is our reality, we should reshape this familiar top-down structure to smooth the sharp edges.

To do this, HR has to be fluid and not stagnate or isolated. Remember: If a department has people in it, then it needs HR.

We can't afford to keep performing from an outside-in perspective. When we do that, we're not living up to our capacity, and we aren't being as fully effective as we should be organizationally. Intentionally working within all departments and across all levels of staff will allow HR to flourish. This isn't theory. It's attainable, and it positions HR to be the business partner that it wants to be.

Take some steps to fight being exhausted and busy. Turn the corner and get full yourself. After you do this, jump back in and fill the buckets of the employees throughout your company. When you do this, doors open and you start seeing the talent, strengths, and aptitude that people bring to work all the time. They're waiting for someone to tap into all they have to offer. Get full, and never be empty again.

CHAPTER 20

LIFE VS. FUNCTION

EXECUTIVES EXPECT HR PROFESSIONALS to know their field, of course. When I hear this, I'm a bit dumbfounded because that seems so basic. Why would people say this unless they've experienced an HR department that was underequipped? We can't afford to be a profession that fakes it until we make it.

I understand that the field of human resources is vast. That's really an understatement. Generalists in HR need to have the ability to perform strategically, be the legal watchdog of the organization, act as the counselor and psychologist for employees, and shine as the champion of the company culture. By the way, all of those attributes need to happen concurrently without a set structure or time frame, and those roles and responsibilities don't capture all that HR is expected to own. Every profession has many attributes and variances, but few have as many disjointed roles as HR.

With that diverse framework, it's easy to see how you can know a piece of each area and yet not have a deep knowledge of any of them. Chances are, the area in which you aren't as deep is the area in which your organization will ask you to respond. That situation can be rough and make you feel inadequate. The result may be that the company, tired of being disappointed in your lack of expertise, may use HR less and less over time

There is a way to break free from this "jack of all trades and master of none" reality. However, it requires a radical shift in how HR has been taught and practiced. We need to be **intentional**.

Is that it? Yep. It can't be that easy, can it? Yep again.

I don't mean this to be trite or flippant. However, the majority of people in HR spend much of their time being indirect, vague, and distant. Our fear of impending doom and/or litigation cripples us. Please note that I am not encouraging you to be reckless or cavalier. Keeping liability and risk in check is a key responsibility for HR within organizations. It should be a strength of who we are and what we offer.

How many times have you had an HR situation or interaction with an employee, and you're response sounds like this: "I'm not sure about that. I'll need to get back to you." You were honest with that response, but the moment you returned to your office, another item came up and you forgot to get back with the person you just encountered. Trust me. I used to be this HR practitioner. It was easier to buy some time and delay than it was to face the situation and work through it right at the time it occurred. Having a dodge-and-parry approach to HR isn't effective. It never has been, and yet people are doing it even as you're reading this.

Being intentional in HR means that you have to be knowledgeable in what you do. There can't be an excuse. Having assurance and confidence in what HR does in your organization will establish you as a credible resource who is included in conversations and decisions. If you waver in what you know, then you'll stay in the pattern of being used only when absolutely needed. You'll be a shadow in your company, and that isn't good for you or others.

How can you stay on top of this ever-changing field? Many ways exist that are easy, accessible, and cost-effective. Here are some to get you started.

Be a Voracious Reader

Remember when I noted earlier that most people say that they're "busy"? This is the answer people give when they don't have time to read in addition to doing their regular job. It's not true. You can choose to be a reader and consumer of content just as easily as you can choose not to read. Take in HR material, business books, and other subjects that may honestly pique your interest. As a reader, you will be mentally sharper in your daily activities, and you will also be more well versed in your field.

I have subscriptions to over 80 HR and business blogs that I read regularly. Some of them I scan, and others I pore over each word. I use an aggregator that curates these blogs so I can read them on my time and when I need a mental break from the pace of the day. I also make sure to read at least two non-HR-related books on an on-going basis. I may dive into mystery, science fiction, or a biography (usually about rock musicians).

When I hear people state that they believe in continuous learning, I ask them what they're reading. I know there are many different ways and methods to learn, but reading is usually involved. If they can't answer the question, I encourage them to read. It keeps you current.

Be Visible and Active in Social Media

HR still has an aversion to social media. I hope that this continues to dissipate because we need to realize that even though we may think social media is a waste of time, others don't. People are using a multitude of platforms to connect and communicate. I understand that there is an inordinate amount of noise and fluff in social media. It's easy to get lost in or frustrated with the volume and the relentless pace. To counter this possibility, you need to once again be intentional.

Instead of throwing your hands up and screaming that you don't "get it," step back and learn what works for you. No one says that you have to be active on every single platform that exists. Some forums disappear even before you can get engaged and active. A suggestion to consider is to set aside some time to research which platforms HR people who are comfortable and consistent in social media use. See who posts regularly on LinkedIn, and read what they're saying. Find someone on Twitter who shares content of others, not only their own work. You can find people who are very good at communicating on Instagram, Snapchat, and the other platforms.

Social media is a way to communicate and learn. Nothing more grandiose than that. You need to be where the thought leaders of our field play. Figure out your capacity for participation and jump in.

Be Alive!!

This last suggestion is the differentiator missing in HR. We should all be functional experts in what we do. When you look at people in the trades, they are expected to be fluent and skilled in the service they provide. We pay for that expertise and are thankful when people can perform work that we may know from a fringe perspective but that they flourish in.

Our trade is HR. We can't just keep showing up and plodding along with the tactical tasks in our roles. Those may be necessary, but they shouldn't define us. If we looked at what we did as something people would pay for, our view of the value of work we do would improve. To shift our approach we need to bring another level of intentionality to human resources.

I'm geeked about HR!! It's not a show or some facade—it's my belief and my norm. I can't wait to dive into employee situations. I broke the cycle of the "I'll get back to you" response. I look at each interaction as a chance either to bring a solution or to plant some seeds of encouragement to get through difficulty. I know that working with people is tough, but what we've forgotten is that we're people too! Others may look at working with HR as tough because, as humans, we can either be an obstacle or a connector.

We have the opportunity to breathe life into all that we do and into every person we work with. This isn't some platitude; it's the truth. It's a big step to take once you enter this direction in practicing HR. Rest assured that if you are someone who brings life to HR, you'll experience human resources as it was intended to be.

Aren't you tired of just showing up?

Step back, take a deep breath, and then exhale. The next step is yours to take intentionally.

CHAPTER 21

SAFE HAVEN

THE AVERAGE WORKPLACE is fraught with unknowns, idiosyncrasies, and politics. That's just Monday. It's amazing that we are success-ful in navigating the workplace at all. I'm not just talking about HR professionals. I'm talking about employees. The majority of employees come to work every day with the desire to do their best. That might not be what we think about them, but it's true. Since people may be on the defensive either because of their workplace culture or the lack of clarity in their roles, it's no wonder that we are in a constantly moving stream of employee relations issues. Throw in the misconstrued expectation that people should talk only about work-related topics, and you'll realize why we have job security—because work-related topics are rarely what's being talked about. People talk about people. The constant swirl of partial communication, assumed practices, and incessant deadlines are just a few more factors of today's work environment.

We expect each employee to bring his or her "whole self" to work in our motivational posters and annual meeting presentations, but we do our best to limit what that really means. You hear managers regularly complain that their staff members are too dramatic or that they waste their work time talking about personal situations they're facing. Do you know who brings their personal situations to work with them? **EVERYONE!!** So why in the world would we express this old-school nonsense in today's workplace? Are we afraid that someone will share something so shocking, offensive, or awkward? People's lives are an open book on every platform of social media. Bringing that into the workplace is not as out of place as you may think.

Another factor needs to be thrown in the mix here. We don't like everybody we work with. We say we do, but that's just not true. I'm not trying to cast a dark pall on work; I'm merely stating the reality that most HR people quietly whisper about. However, all employees deserve respect. They do. These back hall conversations that slowly erode the morale and culture of leadership teams and overall organizations need to be brought out into the light and ad-dressed openly. Does that mean we pull people aside and say, "So,

Steve, we'd like to tell you how much we don't care for you?" No, it doesn't. That would be awful.

How can we function in environments where so many stressors exist? There is a simple way to do it, but it means that you have to deconstruct how you've learned to practice HR. You need to be the safe haven of the company for all employees. **ALL** employees.

Working with people is difficult. That's a fact. People are messy, complicated, intense, passionate, emotional, and illogical. What we've forgotten is that **WE** are people as well!! When you listen to HR professionals talk, it's as if they're in a constant state of third-person communication. Seriously. HR folks talk as if they have become soulless, sentient beings that look over the masses of people that they have to "deal with." We comment the majority of time on what they're not doing, and make sure to note it either in archaic performance reviews or on disciplinary forms to keep a permanent record. Doesn't this tire you out?

I used to be the kind of HR person who seemed to walk through employees as if they didn't exist because I had to get to work that was "more important" and worth my focus, time, and effort. One day that all changed.

When I was working in the tool and die plant I mentioned in Chapter 9, I started a new practice by going into work using the plant employee door versus going through the front door like everyone else from the office. As I walked in, I had to go past the shipping and receiving department. This is where Tom worked. Tom had been with the company for many years. He was a grumpy guy who often complained about most things in life.

When I walked by to head to my desk, he'd shout, "Hey, Steve!! F--- you!!"

The entire shipping department, including the supervisor, would break into uproarious laughter. I was stunned the first time it happened. I just couldn't believe it. I had very little interaction with Tom and was perplexed. Now, I know that "great HR people" would not have tolerated that. They would have gone to the plant manager or the head of operations to put together a performance improvement plan with a call for sensitivity training that would include a written warning for insubordination. I didn't do that. I kept walking in the same door every day and would wait for Tom to shout his vulgar greeting once again. I would always respond, "Hey, Tom," and walk through to my office.

After two weeks of this, I came back out to the department and went straight to Tom. The moment he saw me he shouted, "Hey, Steve!! F--- you!! What brings you the f--- out here?" I responded calmly, "I came to see you, Tom." There were audible "ooooooh" sounds because his co-workers thought he was about to get in trouble from HR. They had been waiting for this.

"Hey, Tom, what do you do outside of work?"

The question stumped him. He was ready to launch into some further tirade. He collected himself and said, "I bowl."

"Are you any good?"

"GOOD? I'm f---ing great. I have a box of trophies to prove it."

"Doubt it," was my sarcastic reply.

"What??"

"I doubt it, Tom. I think you're someone who is full of hot air and brags about what he's good at, but I can't see it."

"I'll f---ng show you! Come back over here tomorrow when you come in, and I'll prove it."

"Okay, I guess. Whatever," and I walked back to my office. I could hear the vulgarities being spewed as I walked back ignoring every single one.

The next day, I came in the plant door and went straight over to Tom. He pulled out a gigantic box and slammed it on the work bench, and said, "See! Told you I was good!"

He really was good. He carried a 275 average, and the box had to hold 30 trophies at least. Here's where it got fun.

I pulled out one of the trophies and asked how he earned this one. He told me about the tournament, the bowling alley, and how he won. We went through each trophy, and I listened intently to each story. I told him that he proved me wrong and that I appreciated him showing me everything and went off to my office.

The next day I came to work and walked through the plant door past shipping, and Tom yelled, "Hey, Steve, how are you doing?"

The other employees stopped what they were doing. I also stopped, walked over to him, and asked him if everything was okay. He said it was and wished me a good day. I couldn't let this pass. I asked him what had changed for him to greet me differently. He couldn't wait to tell me.

"You're the first person from the office who has paid attention to me in years. Most of these f---ers don't even show their face out here. Then you actually took an interest in something I did, and when I pushed back, you stayed and listened to my stories. I wish that would be how management treated all of us."

Tom and I became very close after that, and he was a champion for me for the staff throughout the plant. I found out about his family and that he was a deacon in his church. I had to laugh when I asked him how he took the weekly offering. "Hey, put your f---ing money in the plate" was how I imagined it.

Tom is like most of the employees in your company. No one takes the time to stop and listen to people about their lives. We're in a mad dash to attend a meeting, to answer an e-mail, or to join a conference call as we blindly pass through the most important aspect of our companies—the humans.

To be a safe haven in HR is something that is needed because your people are aching for someone who will acknowledge them, believe in them, and give them the time of day. It is honestly the best part of being in human resources. Providing a place that is nonjudgmental, open, and empathetic will transform you personally as well as redefine your organization.

Ever since my interaction with Tom, I make sure that the majority of my day is focused on the lives of those I work beside. The result has been amazing. I have very few employee relations issues, and when I do, we have a relationship in which we can talk openly and candidly. It can still be tiring, but it's a reassuring exhaustion. You need to become the safe haven of your company. It really isn't an option.

CHAPTER 22

HAVE A TRIBE

THE FIELD OF HR can be extremely lonely even though you're surrounded by people every day. It can be depressing when we enter a room and people say "Shhhhh," and the room gets silent immediately. (You should really not allow that to happen to you, by the way.) It's easy to feel like an island because of the nature of the work that we do. You serve as a repository for the endless emotional highs and lows of all employees at all levels of the organization, in addition to having to perform the day-to-day duties of your role. We aren't often the ones invited to belong to social groups within the company. People are concerned that their behavior, beliefs, or thoughts might offend us and get them into trouble. It's not true, but it's the stereotype we've earned.

When the majority of your work is spent trying to keep people in line, you can't expect to be included. I don't believe this is how HR should be practiced in the least, but I know that the vast majority of human resources is wrapped in constraint versus allowing people to be themselves. It's ironic because we say we value diversity, but only if it "fits." People are like a beautiful mosaic that is always evolving and changing. They never remain constant or predictable. That's very cool because "people" are our chosen profession.

I spent the first 10 years of my career developing and maintaining a social network in my workplace. Social connection has always come naturally for me. I'm a very social being, and I like to surround myself with people. I know that's not the case for everyone, but because the drive in me is so strong, I felt increasingly isolated at work because people were friendly but only up to a point. One day, a flyer (actual paper and not something electronic) came across my desk. It was an advertisement for a human resources roundtable to be held near my office. It listed the date, time, and place, and I decided to check it out.

At the first roundtable I attended, 12 HR professionals came. There was an agenda, and we all sat around a table, literally. The facilitator had us all introduce each other and then asked if anyone had anything he or she would like to discuss. The remainder of that hour, which had started so positively and welcoming, turned into a vicious gripe fest. I didn't participate much. Afterward, I asked the facilitator if I could talk to her for a minute. She was very well known in the local HR community and had even won awards for her work throughout her career. She looked worn out and beaten.

I didn't want to complain, but I asked if this was the tone of every roundtable. She said that this was one of the better ones. I was floored. I was also disappointed because I desperately wanted to connect with others who practiced HR. I was hesitant to give the roundtable a second try, but I did. I stuck with it, and one day the facilitator called me to tell me she was going out of town. She wondered if I would like to run the roundtable while she was out. I jumped at the opportunity. I told her that I had some stipulations, though, before I'd fill in. I asked for the spreadsheet with the names of all the people who had expressed interest in the HR roundtable. It contained 100-plus names on it, whereas we were averaging only 12 attendees!! This seemed upside down. I also asked permission to change the format and have actual discussion about a topic instead of just an open forum. She agreed and let me take over, um, I mean, step in.

I contacted every person on the spreadsheet and invited him or her to the next roundtable using upbeat language about the topic to encourage each to come. I felt that I would have an overflowing room for sure. That next month 15 people came. Three new people. My ego was a bit bruised, but it was a start. We talked about networking, and I spent the hour making sure we really took time to get to know each other and become connections. They agreed to become connections, and my network began to grow. I asked everyone to invite at least one peer to join him or her at the next meeting. The following month we had 16 people.

The facilitator heard about how I ran the forum from the regulars, and asked if I would mind taking over (for real this time) in her role. I did, and I still run that roundtable 17 years later. We now average between 90 to 100 people a month, and there's no cost to come. I still invite the entire database of people who have expressed interest in attending and even stand outside the building to greet them. Every. Month.

The point of this story is that HR people long to be connected. We are tribal, and I know this isn't a new idea. Being part of a tribe isn't only a concept; it's a reality. People want to be with others. What I learned in taking over and growing the HR roundtable is that our tribe is made up of others in HR. There is a ton of comfort, stability, and joy in having a circle of peers who are your friends.

With social media, that tribe can literally be global. We will be stronger as a profession the more we are connected. You see, **we are better together**.

There's no excuse for practicing HR in isolation. You can join professional HR societies and local HR groups and/or chapters, read HR blogs, and connect on social media platforms with little effort. Yes, this takes time, but the fallout of trying to continue to practice HR alone is devastating over time. We need each other.

There is one point to consider as you develop your tribe. What is your capacity? I mentioned earlier that I'm extremely social. I never tire of meeting new people and asking them to be a part of my professional network. That has led to thousands of connections, and I don't even feel I've scratched the surface. Again, I know that I'm an outlier. You may be more comfortable with a much smaller group of folks to be your HR tribe. That's perfect. I have those tribes as well, and I try my best to connect others in HR with peers so that they can have a hand in establishing their go-to group.

A quote was shared within my closest peer group (my tribe) that perfectly captures how this effort is greater than knowing someone only from a business perspective: *"Find your tribe. Love them hard."*

It's ideal and needed. We are better when we come to terms with the fact that we want to belong and love others. It's okay to say you want to belong, be connected with others, and to believe in HR.

These emotions far exceed anything that could be misused in an inappropriate way. You don't have to start your own HR roundtable to have a tribe, but you do need to be intentional in getting out of your bubble of one and in connecting. Step out and do this. You'll see how much those tribe members will support you and lift you up.

CHAPTER 23

THE WORK OF NETWORKING

DO YOU ENJOY meeting people personally and/or professionally? Does there have to be a compelling reason to make you want to meet others? Is the only reason you meet people because you read a blog post that told you that you need to have a network?

I remember when I first began my career, I heard about how important it was to have a network of people. Like most people, I didn't do it because I did not see any tangible reason to create one. In fact, I don't know one person who had a network when I started in HR. I'm sure they existed, but not in the circles of people I knew. The vast majority of people went to work, did their jobs, and interacted with each other, and it ended there. You could be successful and functional within an organization, so there was no compelling reason to reach out to others.

What is ironic about not building a network early in my career is that I thrive on meeting new people. That's a fact. Whenever I go to a new environment, I reach out to meet people. I really want to get to know who they are and something unique about them. I understand that this may not be for you, and I wouldn't recommend doing it unless you have the capacity to take in more and more folks.

I'm not a collector. Many people who network do so because they have an ulterior motive that is intended to result in a sale of their services or products. When this occurs, people are only scratching the surface of truly connecting, and yet people continue to do this. Recently, a person who was a guest at one of the pizzerias I work at came up to me and said, "You look friendly and are always smiling. Here's my card, I represent … ." I was floored. No name. No introduction. Just a chance to whip out the 30-second sales pitch because he thought this was an effective way to meet other people. I threw his card away.

Networking should have a lasting effect. A percentage of your contacts will always be acquaintances, and that is natural. However, if the majority of people in your network remain only acquaintances, then you're missing out. You need to build and develop relationships with those in your network. This is the key that will have an impact. If you can't tell others about a connection past a rectangular piece of paper, then they really aren't a connection at all. Remember, if you're too busy to make time for others, don't have them in your network, and don't be in theirs. That may sound a bit harsh, but great connections encourage each other. They don't use each other.

The key to networking is to do the work. Having a viable network and being an effective networker should be a mandatory skill for all business people—especially for those in HR. Let me be clear: This is a business skill and not a job-hunting skill. We've lost sight that having a set of go-to people makes us stronger professionals in our roles both within our companies and in our industries.

I was at a chamber of commerce meeting a few years ago when I worked for the architecture/engineering firm I mentioned earlier. I served on a committee that met in downtown Cincinnati. The room was filled with a few familiar faces as well as some new folks. The meeting goal was to encourage businesses to be more connected to the chamber and use its resources. I was a kind of "ambassador" for this committee, and we hoped to generate interest in gathering others to join us.

During the meeting, one of the new attendees raised her hand and asked a question.

"Hi there. My name is Carol, and I'm new to the city, and so is my company. We just moved here from California, and I'm trying to get a lay of the land. I wondered if the chamber could recommend any law firms that I could connect with. I need some help on the business side of things as well as employment law. I don't want a downtown attorney because I just don't trust them. I need someone who wants to meet me, get to know my company, and what we do. Can you help me? I'd love to use a fellow chamber member."

The response that followed dumbfounded me.

"We have a chamber directory that you can purchase that lists all of our members and their services. It costs $200, and I'd be glad to go grab you a copy."

Carol stated she just wanted a few names and didn't need to purchase a directory. I wrote down on a piece of notebook paper, "attorney." The meeting continued, and the chamber staff kept its hard sales pitch going. After 20 minutes or so, Carol raised her hand again.

"Sorry. Just wanted to ask another question, if I could. I'd like to get recommendations for a background screening company too. We're planning on doing some hiring both here and back in California. It'd be great if you had a chamber member who could do national searches for me. Do you have any recommendations?"

"I mentioned before that we have a directory for sale. That's all I can do. We need to move on to the other points of our agenda."

I shook my head in astonishment. I wrote "background screens" below my other note. The meeting continued for another half hour, and people said their goodbyes, grabbed their coats, and got ready to leave. I thought I'd take a chance and reach out to Carol.

"Carol, do you have a second? My name is Steve, and I took some notes about your questions. I have a great law firm I can recommend as well as a background screening company that would easily be able to handle your screens both locally and nationally. Now, the attorney does work downtown, but it is a relationship-based firm that I've personally used for HR issues, and the company I work for has used them for broader representation. Would it be okay for me to contact them and have them contact you? They're just an option, but I wanted to make sure to help you."

She was taken aback a bit by my straightforwardness, but she relaxed and thanked me for helping her. She expressed how disappointed she was by the chamber's response, and I assured her that she just hit the wrong representative. I'd be glad to help her. We exchanged business cards, and then she left.

When I got to my car, I called my attorney connection, Dave, and asked, "Dave, how'd you like some business?"

He exclaimed, "Of course I would!" I told him about Carol and how he needed to be relationship-based to assuage her concerns about his working downtown, and I told him that I wanted him to be the first voice mail on her phone when I hung up. He assured me that he would call and follow up.

I then called Chip from the background screening firm. Please note something here—I didn't do work with this firm myself, but I knew Chip and how good he was. "Chip, do you want some business?" He jumped at the chance, and I explained the opportunity and told him that I wanted him to be the second voice mail on her phone. He said that he'd call right after we finished.

Three days later, I received a call at my office.

"Hi there. This is Steve Browne. How can I help you?"

"Steve, you're the young man I met at the chamber meeting a few days ago. This is Carol."

"Yes, ma'am. How's it going?"

"Well, to be honest, I'm a bit confused. Can you tell me what you do again?"

"Yes, ma'am. I work in HR for an architectural and engineering consulting firm. Did my friends call you?"

"Yes, they did. I met with Dave already, and we've hired his firm to represent us for all of our legal representation. They are very good, and you were right that he was relationship-based, and I really cherish that. I have called Chip, and he's sending me a quote for our background screening business. I'm pretty sure we'll go with his firm as well."

"That's awesome, Carol!! I knew they'd be great resources for you."

"You're in HR, right?"

"Yes, ma'am. Is something wrong?"

"No, I've just never met someone in HR like you. Typically I don't find that HR folks are that connected. You've been a real help. Now, you mentioned that your company does architecture, right?"

"Yes, ma'am."

"Well, could you have one of your architects call me?"

"Sure, what are you looking for?"

"I mentioned that we moved my company to the area from California. What I didn't mention to you or the people at the chamber is that I'm the CEO of the company. We're looking to add 300 jobs here on the east side of town, and I really needed a lawyer and a screening company. We're looking to expand out west as well, and you've been a great help. I'm looking to add several manufacturing buildings on our property here in Cincinnati, and I'd like to talk to someone at your firm about this. Can you make that connection for me as well?"

"Yes, ma'am. I'd be glad to."

She thanked me again, and I walked back to the architecture department and asked the lead architect, "Hey, Gary, how'd you like some business?"

Carol's company hired our firm and did several projects with us for several thousand dollars over an 18-month period. Carol also hired the legal firm and background screening company I recommended. It brought both firms several thousand dollars' worth of business as well.

HR people are hesitant to reach out and meet others. This is ironic because we are in the people business. This isn't a factor of being extroverted or introverted. It is a factor of not seeing the value of taking the time to connect with others.

It's time to change this and start building your network within your field with other HR professionals—and others—who could end up being great business and/or personal connections. Just so this isn't overwhelming, make a commitment to connect with one or two new people in HR. Send them a LinkedIn request with a personalized invitation. Be active on social media platforms such as Twitter, Instagram, Facebook, and Snapchat, and connect with other HR folks. Share HR blogs you read with others. Go to events and find a few people you don't know, and take the time to intentionally meet them.

Be content with adding just a few people to your network each week. If you have a larger capacity, meet more people. However, commit to making sure they are connections and not collections. You'll be a stronger HR professional when you have others around you who can encourage you and share their experiences and knowledge.

I hope you understand how much of a difference this will make. It will be some of the most meaningful work you'll ever do.

CONCLUSION

On Purpose

HR. It's the best and most challenging profession one can do. It has a mix of highs and lows that can occur within the same hour depending on the situation you're addressing. There is a constant swirl of emotions that can consume and overwhelm you from both yourself and the people with whom you coexist. The laws and regulations you need to understand and comply with never remain the same. In fact, when changes occur, people lose their mind and are sure that the end of the world will surely occur when the next law has to be implemented and followed in the workplace. There honestly isn't a roller coaster in the world that can keep up with the ebbs and flows of human resources.

That is why the field remains so relevant and awesome!!

People state that they want variety in their work. We have it. People want an opportunity to add value and make a difference in the work they perform. We have that. People would love to have a job where they can work and influence an organization from the top to the bottom. We have that. Isn't that incredible?

I want to leave you with one final perspective to keep you grounded and positive about who you are and what you can do in HR. If you maintain this position and hold true to it, I guarantee that you'll have a long career in HR and enjoy it the entire time you practice.

Focus on others first and always.

This isn't some fluffy feel-good idea. It's a viable way to influence business and affect the bottom line. The difficulty is that it takes a change in our mindset. Focusing on other people is contrary to the "what's in it for me (WIIFM)" mantra. Determining motivators for each person isn't practical or even possible.

However, spending time—uninterrupted time—with others at all levels of an organization is priceless and a differentiator. Why?

It's simple. People don't do it now. Companies, especially at the executive level, feel that when you spend time with people you're "wasting time" because things aren't "getting done." They're wrong.

There is **NOTHING** more valuable and long lasting than investing time in others.

It's difficult to practice HR in this manner because we are surrounded by a society that is self-centered. The majority of communication and interaction is predicated on how many views, likes, retweets, etc., you get. People are constantly staring down at some form of technology to see if someone notices them. That tells you that they have a felt need and desire to be acknowledged, and it's up to us in HR to get them to break from the soft glow of a screen and look up to interact with other humans.

You have to understand that if you take on an "others-focused" effort, you will be going against the flow, which you really need to do to thoroughly enjoy HR (author's biased opinion). Having this focus on an ongoing basis gets tiring, and it's easy to get discouraged, but it's worth it. You have to trust me on this. Organizations, and senior management, are looking for ways that HR can be a business partner, and that can happen only if you're willing to put on your waders and step in the stream to walk against the current.

Focusing on employees also means taking a leap of faith that it will work, and this goes against our nature of being risk averse as a profession. We can no longer be timid. We have to be professionals who practice HR on purpose.

Employees are yearning for an advocate who will genuinely take the time to meet them, listen to them, care for them, and work with them. People want to perform, and they will do better when they know that someone is there for them. You can be this advocate by showing supervisors how to more consistently approach people as humans and not as task fulfillers.

Will you join me? Will you be a person who is no longer re-luctantly in HR and become someone who is passionate and thrives?

I know we can alter the HR landscape and make what we do rele-vant and desired by organizations. I'll be looking for you and will be a willing partner to encourage you, walk alongside you, and make human resources rock—the way it should!!

Every. Day. On purpose.

INDEX

ABOUT THE AUTHOR

AN ACCOMPLISHED SPEAKER, WRITER, AND THOUGHT LEADER ON HUMAN RESOURCE MANAGEMENT FOR MORE THAN 30 YEARS, STEVE BROWNE IS DEDICATED TO CONNECTING THE GLOBAL HR COMMUNITY AND HELPING IT LEARN AND GROW TOGETHER.

Browne has held HR roles in various industries, including manufacturing, consumer products, professional services, and restaurants. He is a member of the Society for Human Resource Management (SHRM) Board of Directors and has been a Membership Advisory Council representative for the North Central Region of SHRM and a past Ohio State Council Director. He facilitates a monthly HR roundtable, the weekly HR Internet forum "HR Net," and a nationally recognized HR blog, Everyday People (www.sbrowne.hr.com).

ADDITIONAL SHRM-PUBLISHED BOOKS

View from the Top: Leveraging Human and Organization Capital to Create Value
Richard L. Antoine, Libby Sartain, Dave Ulrich, Patrick M. Wright

California Employment Law: An Employer's Guide, Revised & Updated for 2017
James J. McDonald, Jr.

101 Sample Write-ups for Documenting Employee Performance Problems: A Guide to Progressive Discipline & Termination, Third Edition
Paul Falcone

Developing Business Acumen SHRM Competency Series: Making an Impact in Small Business HR
Jennifer Currence

Applying Critical Evaluation SHRM Competency Series: Making an Impact in Small Business HR
Jennifer Currence

Touching People's Lives: Leaders' Sorrow or Joy
Michael R. Losey

From Hello to Goodbye: Proactive Tips for Maintaining Positive Employee Relations, Second Edition
Christine V. Walters

Defining HR Success: 9 Critical Competencies for HR Professionals
Kari R. Strobel, James N. Kurtessis, Debra J. Cohen, and Alexander Alonso

HR on Purpose: Developing Deliberate People Passion
Steve Browne

A Manager's Guide to Developing Competencies in HR Staff
Phyllis G. Hartman

Tips and Tools for Improving Proficiency in Your Reports
Phyllis G. Hartman

Developing Proficiency in HR: 7 Self-Directed Activities for HR Professionals
Debra J. Cohen

Manager Onboarding: 5 Steps for Setting New Leaders Up for Success
Sharlyn Lauby

Destination Innovation: HR's Role in Charting the Course
Patricia M. Buhler

Got a Solution? HR Approaches to 5 Common and Persistent Business Problems
Dale J. Dwyer & Sheri A. Caldwell

HR's Greatest Challenge: Driving the C-Suite to Improve Employee Engagement and Retention
Richard P. Finnegan

Business-Focused HR: 11 Processes to Drive Results
Shane S. Douthitt & Scott P. Mondore

Proving the Value of HR: How and Why to Measure ROI, Second Edition
Jack J. Phillips & Patricia Pulliam Phillips

SHRMSTORE BOOKS APPROVED FOR RECERTIFICATION CREDIT

Aligning HR & Business Strategy/Holbeche, 9780750680172 (2009)

Becoming the Evidence-Based Manager/Latham, 9780891063988 (2009)

Being Global/Cabrera, 9781422183229 (2012)

Best Practices in Succession Planning/Linkage, 9780787985790 (2007)

Calculating Success/Hoffmann, 9781422166390 (2012)

Collaborate/Sanker, 9781118114728 (2012)

Deep Dive/Horwath, 9781929774821 (2009)

Effective HR Management/Lawler, 9780804776875 (2012)

Emotional Intelligence/Bradbury, 9780974320625 (2009)

Employee Engagement/Carbonara, 9780071799508 (2012)

From Hello to Goodbye/Walters, 9781586442064 (2011)

Handbook for Strategic HR/Vogelsang, 9780814432495 (2012)

Hidden Drivers of Success/Schiemann, 9781586443337 (2013)

HR at Your Service/Latham, 9781586442477 (2012)

HR Transformation/Ulrich, 9780071638708 (2009)

Lean HR/Lay, 9781481914208 (2013)

Manager 3.0/Karsh, 9780814432891 (2013)

Managing Employee Turnover/Allen, 9781606493403 (2012)

Managing the Global Workforce/Caliguri, 9781405107327 (2010)

Managing the Mobile Workforce/Clemons, 9780071742207 (2010)

Managing Older Workers/Cappelli, 9781422131657 (2010)

Multipliers/Wiseman, 9780061964398 (2010)

Negotiation at Work/Asherman, 9780814431900 (2012)

Nine Minutes on Monday/Robbins, 9780071801980 (2012)

One Strategy/Sinofsky, 9780470560457 (2009)

People Analytics/Waber, 9780133158311 (2013)

Performance Appraisal Tool Kit/Falcone, 9780814432631 (2013)

Point Counterpoint/Tavis, 9781586442767 (2012)

Practices for Engaging the 21st Century Workforce/Castellano, 9780133086379 (2013)

Proving the Value of HR/Phillips, 9781586442880 (2012)

Reality-Based Leadership/Wakeman, 9780470613504 (2010)

Social Media Strategies/Golden, 9780470633106 (2010)

Talent, Transformations, and Triple Bottom Line/Savitz, 9781118140970 (2013)

The Big Book of HR/Mitchell, 9781601631893 (2012)

The Crowdsourced Performance Review/Mosley, 9780071817981 (2013)

The Definitive Guide to HR Communications/Davis, 9780137061433 (2011)

The e-HR Advantage/Waddill, 9781904838340 (2011)

The Employee Engagement Mindset/Clark, 9780071788298 (2012)

The Global Challenge/Evans, 9780073530376 (2010)

The Global Tango/Trompenaars, 9780071761154 (2010)

The HR Answer Book/Smith, 9780814417171 (2011)

The Manager's Guide to HR/Muller, 9780814433027 (2013)

The Power of Appreciative Inquiry/Whitney, 9781605093284 (2010)

Transformative HR/Boudreau, 9781118036044 (2011)

What If? Short Stories to Spark Diversity Dialogue/Robbins, 9780891062752 (2008)

What Is Global Leadership?/Gundling, 9781904838234 (2011)

Winning the War for Talent/Johnson, 9780730311553 (2011)